714

Books by Sheila Burnford

THE INCREDIBLE JOURNEY

THE FIELDS OF NOON

THE
FIELDS OF
NOON

(Every)

SHEILA BURNFORD

THE

FIELDS OF

NOON

An Atlantic Monthly Press Book

LITTLE, BROWN AND COMPANY · BOSTON · TORONTO

QH81
B89

Some of these stories have appeared in the *Atlantic, Maclean's,*
and *Punch*.

ATLANTIC-LITTLE, BROWN BOOKS
ARE PUBLISHED BY
LITTLE, BROWN AND COMPANY
IN ASSOCIATION WITH
THE ATLANTIC MONTHLY PRESS

for Claire Franks — "Frankie"
without whom the fields would have lain fallow
and journeys be left forever untaken

The morning drum-call on my eager ear
Thrills unforgotten yet; the morning dew
Lies yet undried along my field of noon.

But now I pause at whiles in what I do
And count the bell, and tremble lest I hear
(My work untrimmed) the sunset gun too soon.

ROBERT LOUIS STEVENSON
The Morning Drum-Call

Contents

CONTENTS

THE
FIELDS OF
NOON

Canadian Spring

OUR heralds of spring in northwest Canada bear no resemblance to the traditional and seldom inspire the poet within us: no primroses, lambs, or forsythia here, no tender green over the earth and soft unfolding buds. Instead we have the icebreaker battering a channel through the ice cap, smelt running in snow-swollen creeks, frost boils erupting on the roads, municipal drains backing up, and finally an inch-by-inch clearing of the snowdrifts in the garden until the exhausted daffodils push their way through the ironbound earth at last — in June. One's whole soul cries out for spring hats and blossom, new-mown grass, the mayfly hatch, the first young tender morels; instead one pokes ineffectually with a stick at overflowing gutters, yearns over the etiolated narcissus brought up from the cellar, and plucks not primroses but long-lost overshoes and last year's oyster shells from the snow receding at the porch.

In the first week of May, Susan and I reach the peak of delayed-spring frustration, and on a morning when the returning geese fly low over the city in an exultant, baying, clamorous pack, we receive their message especially loud and clear, for we are on our way to Whitefish, to the little hunting cabin on the shore of a lonely, hill-ringed lake, peaceful and timeless: Susan to paint and I to potter; Raimie, my Labrador, to escort us and investigate possible strange noises in the night. We have discarded our families for the weekend.

The track down the hillside to the cabin turns into a fast-running creek at this time of year, carrying off the melting snow from the hills, but the ground is hard and frozen, and the car coasts down in a childishly satisfying welter of flying spray. We leave it in a clearing, load ourselves up like pack mules, then walk or stagger the last quarter of a mile. The trail winds through spruce and poplar, the branches interlaced overhead, and always I come upon the little cabin crouched by the water's edge long before I am prepared for it, so secretly does it seem to camouflage itself against the background of trees. Weather-beaten and gray, wearing its roof and chimney slightly askew, its one half-lidded eye bleary from the winter's gales, it huddles like some shabby, eccentric old woman on a park bench in spring, blinking in the sunshine; and around her skirts, instead of cheeping sparrows, the peaty brown snow creeks make little murmurous singing sounds.

We open the door, and then, as quickly as possible,

the window, when the familiar stuffy, sun-baked smell of mouse nests, straw, waders, and mud-encrusted gunnysacks hits us. The boats are stored there, and we haul out the light punt, then the heavy freight canoe, and a tangled mass of decrepit reed blinds — all the paraphernalia of last fall's hunting; sweep out the first layer of powdered mud and little fluffy piles of duck and partridge feathers; then, lastly, after tossing for the victim, out go all the visible mouse corpses, hurled into the bush, from where they are conscientiously retrieved by the dog and returned to the steps. We leave the door and windows open to the cold sweet northern air; then, mutually unenthusiastic about housework at any time, we call it a day and sit on the wooden steps, at peace with the world, a bottle of beer apiece, so sheltered from the wind and warm in the noon sun that we take off our heavy sweaters and roll up our shirt sleeves.

Almost immediately the cabin's own particular chipmunk appears on the lower branches of an ash, rather leaner than usual after the winter, but recognizable at once by his unusually stubby tail and exuberant personality. He resumes the teasing of the dog from where he left off last November, chattering excitedly. Raimie rises to his baiting like a trout to a fly and is soon reduced to hysterical, impotent rage, until at last the chipmunk becomes a little too bold and is chased up a flue pipe lying under the cabin. A brief but blessed silence follows, until Raimie's eyes close and the next round starts. This has gone on for years.

The ice is going out on the lake, and there is open water before us for about a hundred yards from the shoreline, edged by a new high bank of turf and reeds built up through the winter by ice pressure. The marsh water close in reflects a sky pierced with reed stalks and patterned with a faint constant movement of infinitesimal bubble rings, but out beyond the channel little rippling waves lap greedily against the ice stretching across the lake to the far shore — gray, sodden ice, heavy with age, the darkness of the imprisoned water lying shadowlike a few inches below the surface. There is no hint of green yet in the hills beyond — rather, a quickening of purple; and the three long plumes of the waterfall are vivid and white even at this distance.

The first frog chorus tunes up in the bulrushes a few feet from where we sit, and the mallards who were disturbed at our coming return in quacking pairs to the open water. Four whistlers pass like children's bath toys drawn on a string, line astern, three drakes and a demure little hen leading. One drake is courting extravagantly, head bobbing and turning from side to side to a slow beat of six, then a fantastic arching of neck to twist his head back down the length of his body; but the little hen is not impressed by these contortions and swims on unheeding. The other two watch admiringly, then suddenly rise in unison and fly off with faint despondent cries; and so relieved by their departure apparently is the hen that she turns and acknowledges at last her exhibitionist suitor. They glide and posture in an endless fascinating ritual, the handsome drake in shining black and white, the drab little hen.

A long raft of ice and twigs sails by in a sudden gust of wind, with six mallard passengers aboard; sober and serious as priests on a cruise ship, they stare solemnly as they glide by, all heads turning together. The dog, inquisitive about our laughter, picks his way on heaving planks down to the water's edge, but is taken off guard by the sudden splash of an equally surprised muskrat and slips on the precarious plank, so that his hindquarters slide into the water and he hangs on with scrabbling forepaws. I help him up, because he is nine years old and not so agile, but I laugh so much that he is offended; he shakes his coat, soaking us with moody satisfaction, then disappears into the bush. I know that he will not go far, but will return stealthily and take up position concealed by some bush or tree so that he can keep me within range; and I know that if I turn suddenly I will be able to catch him at it, to his embarrassment — but not this time, for I am feeling a little guilty.

I make amends with a piece of cheese when we settle down on the steps again to eat our lunch — satisfying hunks of homemade bread and cheese, dill pickles, and another bottle of beer to celebrate our weekend emancipation. Redwings chatter in the mountain ash above, chatter in a desultory way, rather as we do ourselves, with long silences savored peacefully between their observations. The frog activity is dying down, but the muskrats are suddenly busy, the V of their wake spreading in the still water close to shore, preoccupied, bewhiskered little faces forging through the reeds. More ducks flight in and settle on the larger ice floes, preening themselves, their cheerful garrulity suddenly silenced when an osprey appears overhead and hovers watchfully. They rise in a body and circle, rising and falling uneasily, until the hawk drifts off down the shoreline on an eddy of wind, effortless as a feather.

Now the wind rises and falls too, sighing through the topmost pine branches, and all around is a chorus of protesting creaks and groans of trees bearing the chafing weight of others uprooted in the winter gales and fallen against them. I am very content; lambs, primroses, and sprays of blossom are suddenly revealed as banal, hackneyed manifestations before this northland subtlety. I find myself filled with pity for the unfortunate masses who must wait another year before picking their next daffodil.

Susan settles down in a protected dip with easel

and paint box and all the colorful clutter of a painter.
She will be lost to the world for the next three
hours. I whistle to Raimie, and we strike off from
the trail into the bush, where the snow has receded,
walking softly on a carpet of damp brown leaves;
through the willow and alder clumps, whippy with
new life, striking like a lash across the unwary face;
over the mossy, rotting deadfalls; and around the
impenetrable branches of new-fallen jack pine, the
needles still dark green, the last desperate growth
of cones in rubbery clusters like brown sea snails;
between towering spruce and white pine; through
enchanting sunlit clearings of terraced rock slabs,
covered in pinky-gray lichen and long trailing ten-
drils of twinflower — the stems and leaves are brown
now, but at the angle of each geometrically perfect
pair is a minuscule of green. The surrounding moss
is ankle deep, beautiful hummocky moss, and however soggy it may be within, I cannot resist it; I
throw myself down and try to count the uncount-
able flowerets in a quarter inch. My eyes are on a
level with a ledge of rock; caught below an overhang is a papery garter-snake skin, old, yet still
clearly patterned and wonderfully supple, over two
feet long. I tie it in a neat bow on Raimie's tail;
he is not amused, but suffers it as a collar instead.

I meander along the banks of a trout-brown creek,
sun-dappled until it winds through the dark gloom
of a cedar swamp, the twisted, agonized roots and

branches of the giant fallen trees forming a dark dramatic frieze against the new vivid green of the living spruce beyond. The cold strikes suddenly, for the sun cannot penetrate the intertwined vaulting, and even the creek contributes to the brooding eeriness with weird shapes and fantastic grottoes sculptured from the overhanging ledges of ice.

Suddenly Raimie hurtles past, nearly knocking me into the creek, tail streaming, nose to the ground like a hound. He disappears into the thick undergrowth, his golden coat flashing momentarily in a patch of sun, and as I walk on, his quarry erupts from the bush across my path, then pauses to look back, upright on his haunches, still as a plaster rabbit on a suburban lawn, save for his twitching nose. A mighty crashing heralds Raimie's reappearance, and the rabbit bounds off with a flash of full white winter trousers, contrasting absurdly with his neat tan summer coat. My idiot dog will now make the full round of the rabbit's tracks before starting off on this new line, for he stubbornly refuses to hunt on anything but scent, and I have often wondered what would happen if a rabbit decided to run in ever-diminishing circles.

Of course, Raimie should not be hunting rabbits — or even his dearest enemy, the groundhog, for that matter — for he is a gundog, trained, with nine years' wisdom and experience. *He* knows that, and *I* know that, but after several argumentative years

together, we long ago arrived at a mature and satisfactory compromise: in return for shouldering a
few extra duties (watchdog, childsitter, sled dog,
juvenile circus performer, losthamster retriever, plus
the full-time summer job of bear-scare on mush-
rooming expeditions), he may hunt for his own
amusement, without let or hindrance, throughout
the year until September 15, or such time as the
upland game and wildfowl season opens, when he
must immediately put aside all temptation and revert
forthwith to his professional capacity of model gundog. It was his terrible misfortune to be born a
scion of the great Shedd of Arden, to spring from
a long illustrious line of field trial champions and
inherit the nose of an inspired cross between radar
and a divining rod — and yet be subject for his lifetime to the whim of a woman-wielded gun. Any
other dog would have a nervous breakdown, and
because of his most generous acceptance of the in-
equalities of fate, I feel I must make allowances.

He never betrays our agreement, and would not
acknowledge a rabbit if he fell over one during the
shooting season; and even my hunting companions,
critical field trial purists though they are, admit
that it would be difficult to find his equal as a
retriever of lost and given-up birds, or a heart more
eager and willing for work, whatever the conditions.
Their only accusation, in fact, is that he smells
faintly — but deliciously, I contend — of Schiap-

arelli's "Shocking," just behind the ears. He is the only dog I know who has been confronted with eleven mallards down in a treacherous, ice-fringed Manitoba slough and has set to work, systematically and entirely under his own directive, to bring them in (his mistress watching admiringly but uselessly, as her boots were leaking), then disappeared into the surrounding countryside, to reappear at ten-minute intervals with four more crippled birds. And only a woman owner could appreciate the gallantry of his compliment in bringing all fifteen birds to me, even though I had not fired a shot — a dogless companion being responsible for the massacre. And I know of no sight more fascinating than to watch him paddle painstakingly back and forth across a suspect area of water, submerging his head at intervals, until he finally dives straight down and comes up with a live but suicidally minded duck.

If I have digressed, it could be suspected that I dote on him.

I leave the creek to come out from the darkness of the bush at the edge of a field, part of a long-abandoned fox farm, and there, less than a hundred yards away, in a dip before the sagging barn, is a black bear. We stare at one another in mutual horror for a long second; then he turns and bolts across the field, galloping so fast that his back legs cross over his front ones, and disappears into the far trees. But that is the direction I want to go in as well, back to the lake, and I don't feel entirely happy about bears, and however antisocial this one may be, perhaps he has a mother or a cousin or a sister (with cubs) who isn't. I call my moral support away from his rabbit hunting and hear the reassuring sounds of his coming almost immediately. He arrives, panting, with beaming eyes and half a yard of pink tongue lolling out of a grinning mouth; I gather he has had a wonderful time. I am delighted, even more than usual, to see him. I am interested to see him sniff the wind as we cross the field, and the ridge of hair rise along his back, but he trots along beside me unconcerned; and so, of course, am I — now.

Susan has had a satisfying afternoon as well; two canvases are propped against the backs of chairs, she has found the glove she lost last fall in the bush, and has seen two deer, one mink, and a flock of geese. We sit on the steps again before dinner, loath to come in until the last possible moment, and watch a spectacular sunset flaming in wild, windblown ragged clouds. The air below is still and soft and full of evening sounds: wings whistling overhead, throbbing frog chorus from the reeds, chickadees, and the solitary falling cadence of a white-throated sparrow far back in the bush; little whispers of wind rustling the dead brown bulrush spikes; and always the soft melodious tinkling of shifting ice in the background; coy bridling giggles of mallard hens in the next bay, protesting their virtue to the hoarse excited quacks of their swains; the occasional caustic comment of a raven. We sit there until the loons cry in the gathering darkness and the cold drives us into the snug, stuffy warmth of the cabin.

We have partridge for dinner, succulent gamy partridge shot in a Saskatchewan bluff last fall, marinated and cooked in homemade wine from a local Italian producer; Burgundy jelly from the Trappists in Quebec; and wild rice that grew along these shores only last year, dark and fragrant with woodsmoke from the Indians' fires across the lake. We drink the remainder of the wine — a muscatel, says the sticking-plaster label on the gin bottle, with a surprisingly pleasant though elusive bouquet (a quality enhanced perhaps by the fact that our wineglasses once contained anchovy paste).

We play featherheaded chess until our eyes will no longer stay open and we realize that we are dozing between moves. Raimie is already asleep on a sagging cot, muzzle resting on a headless decoy, his nostrils twitching — dreaming of rabbits, probably. I lie awake in the darkness for a while, zipped into the cocoon of my sleeping bag, listening to the sighs and creaks of the wooden framework; there is a soft, intermittent scratching on the roof, which I finally identify as a scraping branch; outside there are faint little plops in the water, and a closer, intensified tinkling of the ice, which must mean that the wind is shifting.

In the middle of the night I waken with a sudden wide-awake alertness, almost as though someone had called me by name, but I hear nothing — only the sound of Raimie's tail thumping on the cot when he hears me sit up. I get out of bed and stand by the open door, looking out across the lake; a star is hanging low over the hills, and when the moon appears from a bank of clouds the lake is bright before me, half a mile or more of shining water triumphing over the sinking ice. And as I stand there I realize that the wind is warm and soft and full of promise — the promise of the northland spring, fulfilled at last in the silent, vanquished ice.

Walking: Its Cause,
Duration and Effect

O F all the precepts instilled into me from early childhood in Scotland, none has remained more firmly to this day than come rain or shine, hell or high water, no able-bodied person should spend all day indoors: if not actually immoral, it was a Very Close Thing. Once outside, if not otherwise actively engaged, one should go for a Good Walk. This attitude was, of course, endorsed to the hilt by the canine elders of the family. One graduated, therefore, from being taken for one's good daily walks, accompanied by these despots, to accompanying them on their walks by one's goodself alone. There would be a wholesale emigration of North American dogs to Scotland if they knew the conditions that exist there for them: wonderful walks, at least twice a day, in a damp, smell-enhancing climate; three or four miles, up hill and down dale, uncollared, unleashed — for I have no reason to believe that the gumbooted feet of Scotland's young are not still kicking their way through the puddles and squelching across the moors for the good of their souls and the pleasure of the family dogs. Those gumboots . . . My children, looking at my photographs one day, remarked that we never seemed to wear anything else, and did we even wear them in bed? For they had come across a photograph of me standing on a hillside in pajamas, with, of course the ubiquitous gumboots on my feet. When I explained that I was on my way to the beck, or creek, and that when we stayed with my cousins in Cumberland we used to immerse ourselves in it before breakfast, they looked at me as though I had partaken in some strange prehistoric rite.

Some families enjoyed walking together, or in pairs; not ours: my brother, having first found out what direction I was going in, would take his share of dogs and go off in the opposite; my father took his friend the Sheriff for what he called a "tramp;" . . . where they tramped to nobody knew. The Sheriff always seemed to be hurrying to catch up from his two paces to the rear, and it was generally supposed that my father snapped his fingers and said "Heel, sir!" every now and then to encourage him. My mother said that if she could count nothing but the miles she had walked to and from church in her childhood they would take her halfway round the globe, and she flatly refused to walk anywhere nowadays except around the golf course with her favorite caddy, Dugald, trotting at her heels. Except on Sunday, when the golf course was not open, and then my heretic mother, the only true Scot among us, would put her shameless, unwalking feet up and settle down for the afternoon with a novel and some close study of next week's racing form — while the rest of Scotland poured out for the traditional Sunday walk. Brought up in the strictest Presbyterian household, where Sunday was a joyless day spent listening to ministers of the yawning abyss, wrath and gloom school and the lightest literature allowed was Foxe's Book of Martyrs, she reveled in the comparatively sybaritic Sundays that were hers now through marriage into the Church of England. "There but for the grace of your father go I," she said happily one day in the Western Highlands, watching the long procession in its Sabbath black straggling over the hill to the uncompromising varnished deal interior of the local church, and the uncompromising oratory of its minister, who held little hope for the eternal prospects of the human race as he found it in this congregation, and considered all pleasure a sin.

But my mother's emancipation did not extend to her children: she had duly served her walking time, we must serve ours. Wet days, dry days, muddy days, blizzard days we walked; and all over Scotland the pattern was the same, particularly on Sunday, when the ranks were swelled by the heads of the households and the weekend visitors — doors opening and the walkers walking forth before the cooling memories of after-church roast beef. (How strange it must have looked from some celestial viewpoint: like an indeterminate ant colony . . . or what a fascinating picture it would make for one of those motion studies — lines zigzagging to and fro, up and down, in some pointless abstract pattern.) The purists, the weekend walkers, set forth with heads and hearts up and chests out, knobbly ash walking sticks clenched in swinging hands; the Sunday strollers, to-the-cemetery-and-back or tea-with-Aunt-Agnes, went in groups, their furled umbrellas suspended from a wrist strap over their respectable black gloves; then the dour, preoccupied whippet-walkers, their minds on next Saturday's race, stickless save for a possible twig between the teeth, their wide-collared dogs slipping along like medieval wraiths on six inches of lead. Then there were the eccentrics, like the jog-trotting Colonel of the Dandie Dinmonts and malacca swordstick, the loping Games Mistress in lacrosse boots, pushing her bicycle in the basket of which sat a panting pug, or some of the hairier kilted ones, with shepherds' crooks and city voices. And then, of course, there were the day-in-day-outers — the children, the gumbooted habitués, who twirled, dangled or dragged their walking sticks, and it mattered not what kind as long as it had a curved handle.

We could not possibly walk without curved handles to our sticks — invaluable for hooking round the necks of recalcitrant dogs, pulling down branches, rattling along the palings of St. Bride's, prodding; one could practice golf strokes, or ice hockey when the river froze; one could, one supposed, brandish the stick menacingly should a menacing situation arise — or thrust it through an enemy's bicycle spokes. Once mine fended off the vicious wing blows of a swan being rescued from the frozen backwaters; another time I hurled it like a boomerang at a stoat intent upon a nerveless rabbit — but, being me, of course I hit the rabbit instead and knocked it out cold. Fortunately the stoat was so amazed at this performance that I was able to pick the rabbit up before it recovered. The very young among us sometimes sighted along their sticks and said "Boom, boom," or wielded them as a claymore, depending on the historical mood of the moment or the side they had been picked on.

We walked, *how* we walked — so conditioned by custom were we that when we grew out of childhood and gumboots we continued to walk in good stout brogues and adulthood (there were no teenagers then, just children and responsible adults): through the bracken and heather of the West Highland hills, and over the Galloway moors, and miles along the white sweep of beaches at low tide. I remember the Cotswolds in early spring: out of the

whipping wind and into the still sanctuary of the
medieval "wool" churches, those exquisite Gothic
tributes raised by the munificence and devotion of
men who made their fortunes from the fleece of
the Cotswold sheep, their native limestone mellowed
sometimes to a pale gold, holding and yet reflecting
light. We took rubbings from the brasses set into
the flagstones: the wool merchants with their long
pointed shoes and pious hands, side by side with
their wimpled wives, attended often by a devout
kneeling staircase of their many children. Then out
from the church into the thin clear Whitsun sunshine, to sit on a bench outside the inn, with a
tankard of beer and sweet Spanish onions on bread
and cheese, and on across the green rolling country
by bridle path and right of way and Roman road
to the next church, perhaps Saxon or Norman this
time, with a leper's squint, or an especially interesting tympanum. Twelve miles was a pleasant day's
stroll. That I found such pursuits wholly absorbing
and satisfying is a complete mystery to my daughters today. Sometimes I think they think we walked
simply because the wheel had not been invented
then.

Sometimes, as in the Black Mountains in Wales,
we combined walking with mild climbing, and then
we promoted ourselves to climbing boots. These
were rather special: they came from a shop in Lon-
don that outfitted explorers and mountaineers, and

even to look at them made one feel intrepid and Outward Bound. We prepared them for the assault by wearing the boots with the normal quota of socks, then standing in a tub of water. After that we clacked briskly and soggily around Kensington Gardens on their half inch studs. A few days of this treatment, plenty of Dubbin, and they were molded forever into the most perfect foot-fitting contours. I have mine yet. They took me over the Black Mountains, and later the Grampians; over the crags of Cumberland, following fellhounds, and I never had a blister. Though I must in all honesty confess I never had a blister either when we followed those same hounds as children, wearing, naturally, gumboots — what else?

Following these fox (mountain fox) hounds was the supreme test of a walking childhood: it might have been the goal for which one trained from infancy. This was the same rock-clad mountainous country over which that View Halloo that "would awaken the dead" rang, and John Peel hunted his heterogenous pack on Shanks' mare then as we did now, for it is no country for horses. It was a businesslike pack, and hunted not for pleasure but purpose, for there are hungry cubs as well during the lambing season, and foxes will turn to lamb-worrying when for some cyclic reason there is a lack of the small game that normally satisfies them. When we children were there during the Easter

holidays, we used to stuff a hunk of gingerbread
and a couple of apples in our pockets and follow
all day, (and if any Olympic trainers are interested
I can heartily recommend soggy gingerbread for
staying power: it seems to glue body and soul together most comfortingly) — straight up the hillside
to the towering crags and down over the other side,
walking, jog-trotting, walking, trotting, clutching
your thumbs in clenched hands to keep the "stitch"
at bay; short legs trying to keep up with the long
tireless strides of the hill farmers and shepherds who
made up the bulk of the field. The policy was to
reach a vantage point on some peak and watch how
events were shaping; and too often one reached that
peak only to find that the pack was streaming over
the next one and out of sight. I remember shivering
in the rain, and the mist clinging like spiders' webs
to our sodden jerseys as we tried to find our bear-
ings on part of the Roman Way that runs die-
straight across the crest of the range, and from
somewhere in the thick mist beyond the eerie echo-
ing clamor of hounds, on one side the yapping of
the terriers, and from another the huntsman shouting
to someone — all confused and cross-echoing, so that
one was surrounded by meaningless sound in a
nightmare vacuum. And at the end of the day the
long light-headed walk back across the fells, until
we slid down the last screes to Mardale, and the
ancient cottage that my cousins used for holidays,

with its foot-thick walls, crouched against a fold of the hills above the lake; and if it were Saturday night old Hannah might have cauldrons of water on the kitchen range for a bath — the tin one that hung in the barn and doubled sometimes as a punt on the lake. It was set up in the slate-tiled pantry, and we children bathed two at a time in order of precedence.

The fish swim through the cottage now, and water weeds rise from the belfry of the tiny church nearby, for the lake level was raised by a great new dam to supply the North of England. The church was one of the smallest in England, if not actually the smallest: I know that on a Sunday our two families filled it. Uncle Dick, when he was there, played the harmonium for the service — Irish to the core, it was rhythmically impossible for him to stick to strict dirge rhythm in the hymns: our Christian Soldiers marched onward as though bound for Phil the Fluter's Ball, and it was difficult to keep one's feet from tapping as we cheerfully roared our Hosannahs in jig-time. When there was no one available for the harmonium there was a Gramophone, so ancient that it lacked only the white terrier at its gigantic horn. I think we were allowed our choice of the few records, and I vividly remember the panic one Easter with everybody down on their hands and knees searching for the one and only needle, dropped by the Rector's old shaky fingers.

Walking on the continent was an economical form of holiday, with students' cuts on the fares and friendly farmers with hospitable barns. I walked in the Black Forest, but the masses of other walkers there disenchanted me; and I found the lederhosened, dirndled *Wandervögel* rather tiresome in their muscular exuberance and vocal folksiness. I walked and climbed the Dinaric Alps of Jugoslavia in a trance of young love, on the other hand, and loved every inch. I remember being astonished when someone said those hills were stony and arid, and they had nothing good to say for them — my memories were of halcyon heights, over which one trod, light-footed, on a carpet of asphodel . . . (and the *raison d'être* of my state of mind was a German — which must prove something).

The most memorable walking of all was on the High Pyrenees in that long golden summer of 1939. I think that we all knew somehow that it would be the last summer of the carefree years, and that soon we would all be scattered; and we filled every hour of each day, unconsciously storing up memories, like squirrels hoarding nuts before the onslaught of winter. Jill, my companion of many miles of walking, and I based ourselves in the inn on the summit of the Col d'Aubisque; the altitude was about 5600 feet, so we were above the tree line and into the high pastureland where the thin clear air was spiced and fragrant with the profusion of flowers that grew there, nothing exotic, just sweet, common country flowers, rare only in their abundance on the heights, and their enhanced fragrance — iris, poppies, campanula, coltsfoot and lady's-smock, carpets of genista and the golden fire of gorse — all the flowers, in fact, of country childhood. The only sounds, carried for miles in the high stillness, were the ice-cold torrents and waterfalls, and the melodic tinkling of the sheepbells, the sleepy noontime clicking of the cicadas; and the only other human beings we met were the long lean Pyrenean shepherds with their woven blankets slung across one shoulder, and the long traditional crook; in their homespun, different only from the shepherds of home by their goatskin wine gourds and jaunty berets.

We had been young and foolish enough before we left to take a bet that we would not cross over into Spain. Madrid had fallen at last, only a few weeks before, and foreigners were hardly welcome in that chaotic land; however, after a long and devious struggle we secured visas which filled two pages in our passports and seemed to consist mainly of *"no autorizado para . . ."* this and that. The issued numbers on them were so low that we must have been lucky to get them at all. I had a beautiful contour map from the French Alpine Club that showed the mule tracks that zigzagged between the contour lines of the French Pyrenees and across the frontier into Spain. We decided to cross from

Gavarnie: the track wiggled along above the course of the Gave des Tourettes, then down into Spanish Bujaruelo. The walk would be about four or five hours with an easy ascent of about 3000 feet over the Port de Gavarnie, and the only thing to worry about was the vagaries of the mountain weather which can suddenly produce a blizzard or a dense mist out of a clear blue sky. But we were lucky — the only mist rolled back before us in the early morning, and when we crossed the highest point it lay cradled in clouds in the valley far below, so that as we stood there an eagle flew out of it below us; and then, as a wisp of cloud drifted away, the heads of a string of grazing horses suddenly emerged, disembodied, surrealist, on the rim of the great bowl below. It was pleasant walking, canvas and ropesoled espadrilles were just right, except where the snow still lay in drifts; the light winds were cool from the Gabietou and Taillon glaciers above, the glaciers that fed the marrow-chilling mountain streams.

Sometimes we saw a soleless boot or worn-out espadrilles, or other mute evidences of the Republican refugees who had poured over the frontiers after the agony of Catalonia only a few weeks before — the cold must have been cruel beyond endurance then. We ate our lunch unhurriedly, looking down into Spain from our eyrie on a crag, then traversed the last steep slopes, well pleased with ourselves, and crossed the little bridge across the

Ara into Bujaruelo, which consisted of about three hovels. Two barefoot scarecrow carabinieri, the only inhabitants apparently, popped out of the nearest hovel and brandished rifles at us . . . I remember the closeness of the air down here after our rarefied altitudes, and the squalor of the one-time posada, now the guardhouse, the scrawny chickens scratching on the dirt floor, the utter poverty. We spoke kindergarten Spanish, and the guards no English. We showed them our visas, and indicated that we wanted to walk on to Torla, another two hours away, where there should be an inn. Our visas meant nothing: we could cross at Roncesvalles possibly, not here: we must return whence we came. We pointed to the bastion-like range we had just come over, the thousands of feet we must climb again to reach the track: it is dangerous, we said, trying to look like frail Ingleez Misses, for we are already tired, and the sun will sink; we might lose our way — wolves, mist, starvation, etc. They shrugged indifferently. Take us to your Leader, *at once*, we said, switching to not-to-be-trifled-with British Lionesses. They shrugged again: their leader *might* return within a week — if we cared to await his decision . . . and they indicated the flea-ridden hovel with an unmistakable leer, but to Torla: no, non, niente, nein. A night on the bare mountain in a blizzard with genuine wolves would be preferable, we decided. I had the forethought to get one of them to sign the map as evidence for our bet; and then, after we had drunk a tiny glass of thick yellow, indescribably potent liquid, we set out groggily for the return ascent, which looked by now about as inviting as the North Face of Everest. The Guardia escorted us up to the first ridge, their rifles slung over their shoulders — at my urgent request, for I had not fancied their initial horsing around with playful pointings and merry imitations of clicking triggers, and they had complied with extraordinary meekness. We climbed on by ourselves, after shaking hands all round, and I have a vivid picture of them still in my mind: leaning on their rifles in the almost identical pose of the shepherds with their crooks, dwindling below us, as we in turn dwindled to crawling flies above them, until at last they were hidden to sight. It was a long, rough, weary haul back, but so buoyant is youth that I remember little of it, only the welcome lights of the little town of Gavarnie, and trying to keep awake over a particularly superb dinner in a wooden, half-decked room that hung out over the rushing torrent of the river. And I daresay we were up early next morning and on our way to Turon. . . .

The habit of daily walking has been instilled too deeply now ever to be broken. Today the temperature is −10 degrees, and the winds at 25 from the northwest: hardly ideal conditions, yet I know only too well that by three o'clock my conscience will begin to gnaw, and that the dog will contribute to its unease by constant supplication and pacings to and from the door. Sooner or later, a brainwashed robot, I will be in the car with Raimie on the front seat beside me, heading down to the lake to walk out across the ice to the lighthouse and watch the iceboats. Or, and more likely, we will drive up to the bluffs behind Current River on the city boundary, where we have found wonderful winter walking territory: constant sleigh runners have packed the snow hard enough to walk on the surface without snowshoes or skis. This is essential, for Raimie is large and heavy and he is not young any more; he has had one broken shoulder, and this winter dislocated another, so floundering around in deep snow is too hard on him. Even in deepest winter there is always something to see or hear: paw prints, strange wind sculptures of snow, and only now can one appreciate the delicate intricacies of the long curved grasses etched against the snow, and the perfect austerity of the bare trees. Vivid colors by their very scarceness take on a new depth and value: the rich rose of pine grosbeaks in a mountain ash against the perfect whiteness of snow stained scarlet with downcast berry flecks; the flashing brilliance of a blue jay against the dark green of spruce; or the subtle glowing pinkness of birchbark in the low winter sun. I love the sounds of winter too —

the sudden crack of a branch like a pistol shot, the
deep sonic booming far under the iceroads on the
lake, and the soft brushing of heavy snow-laden spruce
branches; but the most exciting sound of all is when
one puts one's ear to the ice above a bend in the
river that is normally deep and turbulent with cur-
rents: the liquid chuckling notes, rushing and sighing
in the ice caverns below, sound like distant music
played behind closed marble doors. And if anyone
wants to hear this music I recommend a scarf or
something laid on the ice first. I always forget and
freeze my ear.

The first year I came to Canada I froze my feet
— always I seem to come back to footwear — and
spent years trying to find adequate winter boots
for this northland country. I tried everything: fur
linings, fiberglass insulation, vacuum insulation, chem-
ically treated insoles with exciting exclamation marks
of heat radiating from them in the mail order
catalogue — everything, and always there was the
excruciating pain of returning circulation, appre-
ciated only to the full exquisite refinements of its
torture by those who have had feet or hands
frozen. Then one year I bought some of the rough,
unadorned moccasins from the Swampy Crees in
northern Saskatchewan: tanned deer or moosehide,
the edges of the long split cuff fold across one another
and are held there by crisscrossed hide thongs. One

pair of felt insoles, one pair of thin socks, and my feet have never lost touch with me since. Their only drawback is that the snow must be powder-dry; and some ultra-fastidious people complain of their kippery smell if I wear them in the house. I suppose that the secret is in having the bones and ligaments of the feet unrestricted and always in contacting movement with the ground through the soft supple soles. Pleistocene man shod himself similarly, and we have not produced better winter footwear since. Or better clothing either, I feel sometimes, for the warmest clothing I know in −20 or −30 degrees includes a deerskin jacket somewhere in the layers. I envy Raimie his warm, practical coat with its long water- and snow-repellent flat hairs, and the thick cozy underfur; the sensible arrangement of his folded self-warming ears; the utilitarian furry feet with the snowshoe webbing between the toes.

Above all I envy him his uncluttered appearance when walking. One day last fall I drove into the bush along a corduroy track, and eventually left the car by an impassable creek. Raimie jumped out, all ready to go; his nose, his only necessary equipment, already twitching. Then I followed, and it took me nearly ten minutes to assemble all the necessary gear for an afternoon's walking in the bush and stow it in the pockets of my jacket, around my waist and over my shoulders. Into the pockets went shells, insect repellent, chocolate, cigarettes, matches, silk scarf, pencil, notebook, and a tired hunk of garlic sausage; attached to my belt were a knife (mushrooms, etc.) and a small prospector's pick (geology); over my shoulders were slung a camera (for photographing mushrooms) and field glasses (distant birds?); I carried in one hand a gun (partridge for dinner), and in the other a chip basket (rocks and mushrooms). I looked like a mobile Christmas tree and was obviously going to be busier than the one-armed paperhanger. But which of my beloved toys could I leave behind? I had already left the blackened pie plate which a prospector had told me I should never be without (any rusty deposits, under uprooted trees, etc., should be panned in the nearest creek), my bottle of Dimethyl-something-oxane for nickel testing, and a trowel. I was stripped down to the barest essentials.* What has happened to me since the days when all I needed was my walking stick with the curved handle, and my gumboots? Is it some deep manifestation of the increasing years, this frantic desire to seize the day in both hands, lose no minute of the wonders that one has so idiotically

---

*If anyone should be a list checker, as I am, and notice a lack, I should say that Kleenex, string, several plastic bags, a safety pin, and a screwdriver were already in my pockets — (I have no idea what the screwdriver is there for), and I never carry a compass: its quivering undermines my confidence, and I cannot believe that anything so abject will not change its mind as often as I change direction — Raimie's nose holds a far steadier assurance: I just tell it that we are "going back to the CAR," then follow.

passed by and left unexplored? I see myself, increasingly hung about with impedimenta, trudging on automatically through the years, until at last I reach senility, and revert, tottering, into unhampered childhood walking.

The Peaceful Pursuit

WHEN Susan, who shares my curiosity and enthusiasm in many mutual interests, first became interested in mushrooms I thought she had really taken the wrong turning this time, and wild horses would not drag me down this dangerous path after her. I humored her, however, and picked, with distaste, any mushroom I encountered in my own mild pursuit of wildflowers and brought it to her to identify; but I firmly declined any invitation to join her in a snack brewed from her repulsive goodies. Like many people I had a classic case of "mycophobia" — a deeply rooted, uneasy feeling that wild mushrooms were toadstools, and belonged to some dangerous half-world: they were rife with superstition, and were "devil's food" or "devil's bread"; indispensable ingredients of a witch's brew, and a Must in every Borgia's recipe book. Calling them "edible fungi" did not help either; at best the ones with red spots on their roofs were inhabited by rather sinister little men with green pointed caps, according to nursery wallpaper nature lore; and even the one Christian legend that included them, however endearing the mental picture it conveyed, left a feeling of considerable doubt — Christ and Peter munching biscuits as they walked and talked; some biscuits were of white flour, some of whole meal, and the crumbs as they fell to the ground turned to mushrooms, the brown ones poisonous, the white ones edible. Yet the only fatal mushroom on the North American continent, according to Susan, was pure white, the Destroying Angel, or *Amanita virosa* (its lethal counterpart in Europe has a pale green cap, and the equally cheerful name of the Death Cap, or *Amanita phalloides*). The whole thing was nerve-wracking; and to court disaster for the sake of eating fried fungus sounded like a gastronomic version of Russian roulette. Susan continued to court disaster with evident enjoyment.

My conversion followed my indoctrination with puffballs. They looked so nice and clean and wholesome, so remote from sinister toadstools, and when I very dubiously tried some, sliced and fried in butter, they were delicious. I borrowed an elementary mushroom book and read that the small puffballs called *Lycoperdon perlatum* could be confused with the dread Destroying Angel in its undeveloped stage by a superlatively stupid and unobservant novice collector: I should, therefore, slice it down the middle first and make sure it was "homogenous." It seemed a reasonable precaution, if I were going to eat any more puffballs, to look up both "homogenous" and *Ama-*

nita; but when I did I found I had to know the parts
of a mushroom in order to understand the descriptive
terminology: I rushed out and picked the nearest
fungi to hand and spread them over the kitchen table.
Now the book told me that mushrooms were divided
into families, like flowers, each with its own distinc-
tive characteristics, and one of the most important of
these was the color of the "spores"; . . . spores were
news to me, but I must take "spore prints." Soon
the kitchen table was covered with a Mad Hatter's
teaparty of glasses inverted over mushroom caps on
paper plates. The results about half an hour later were
most exciting: perfect impressions were left from
under each cap, like the closely radiating spokes of
a wheel, where the spores had dropped off the gills
onto the paper, the colors ranging from pink to
almost black. I was entranced, in thrall, launched:
there was no return.

That was four years and about two hundred mushrooms ago, and I only wish now that I had started
many years ago, for I can think of no pastime more
rewarding than mushrooming, and no outdoor sport
that I will be able to pursue so far down my declining
years — just as long as I can still totter. The exercise
is mild to strenuous, depending upon whether one
bends to pick with bent or straight knees (the latter
is excellent for the waistline); there is all the excitement of the chase, then the reward of eating the
quarry; no expensive clothing or equipment is neces-

sary, just a knife and a chip basket, and the older the clothes the better; there are no problems about where to store or display one's choicer specimens, or what to do with the unwanted ones — one either eats them or throws them away; and if thrown away there is no unsightly pile of rubbish, for they are self-disposable. The soul of a zestful *gourmet-voyageur* is a help; and an equally enthusiastic companion, though not essential, is most pleasant, and reassuring too when one needs an opinion confirmed or denied when trying out a new species. I am fortunate in having Susan, for our respective children are at an age when we have our fair share of free time, and her artist's eye has a professional aptitude for variations in color and texture. We are both blessed with the discriminatory noses of bloodhounds, and this is important in identification, for mushroom smells can vary from sharpening-lead-pencils to freshly ground meal, from frankly fetid to a fragrance as sweet as twinflower, from anise to coal gas. (Sometimes I wish we had a card index of instant smells, as some of the textbook descriptions are quite fanciful: cowslips, artichokes, radish, raw potatoes — it is particularly difficult to remember what a radish smells like, I find.) Another useful piece of equipment if one mushrooms, as we do in deep bush, and therefore bear, country is a dog; dogs seem to give bears fair warning that human beings are about, so that they can gather up their children and depart for safer places. Most dogs thoroughly enjoy the outing anyway, as the slow pace gives them plenty of opportunity to potter around. Raimie has been our official bear-scare for years, and once I even toyed with the idea of turning him into a North American version of the French truffle hound or pig, for he has a wonderfully acute nose. One day we were sitting on a sawdust pile in a woodlot, after picking a batch of *Pluteus* — a rather dull genus that favors old sawdust heaps. I gave one to Raimie to smell, and idly said "Find!" He quartered the area, and I watched the indicator speed of his tail: soon it had reached maximum interest revs, and I walked over — he was pawing at a *Pluteus*. He repeated this success with a few other varieties, but it was not very long before I regretted my ambitions for him; in his enthusiasm (or perhaps subtle revenge for the indignity of being classed with professional pigs) he too often pawed to pieces some succulent specimen just before I reached it, or sat heavily on it instead. I soon released him back to his groundhog and rabbit hobbies.

I am also fortunate that my home in northwest Ontario is within ten or fifteen minutes' easy reach of pastureland, bush trails, hill and lakeshore country — even if I only have six snowfree months to enjoy it in — and consequently there is a wide indigenous range of specimens. But all sections of the country, right across the continent, have their own special varieties; and even the city enthusiast can find endless possibilities in gardens, parks, and waste lots: that bane of the gardener, the "fairy ring" on his velvet lawn, is made up of the little bell-shaped Champignons (*Marasmus oreades*) — excellent in omelettes and stews, or fried; the supply is available from summer to fall, and tastes even better in winter, as they dry particularly well. There are puffballs on lawns and golf courses; some of the short-lived stately Inky Caps (*Coprinus*) grow extensively on well-fertilized lawns, or from invisible stumps or roots under the ground — our best crop in this city comes from the lawns surrounding the Law Courts; and the unmistakable Shaggymane, or *Coprinus comatus*, barrel-shaped when closed, then expanding to a graceful bell, is often found along the roadside in tightly packed soil, or in the lanes dividing back yards in cities. These are the mushrooms that dissolve into an unsightly black mess, and because they are so so soft and ephemeral should be picked in the barrel stage and eaten at once if possible: steamed is best with this consistency, or included in a casserole with breadcrumbs and cheese (and if cast away on a desert island one can use the inky fluid that contains the spores for writing one's S.O.S. in a bottle — it is remarkably unfadable). All the family of *Coprinus* are edible and good — but until one learns to distinguish the one called *atramentarius*, which is really quite easy, it is best to avoid alcohol when eating them, or for some time after, for the combination sometimes produces a hectic flush, fading very soon, but leaving a temporarily pink-tipped nose and ear lobes; this interesting manifestation soon fades too, but another drink within twenty-four hours or so will produce the same Rudolph effect all over again. It is not in any way dangerous, just embarrassing — some of the proprietary medicines used in combating alcoholism work on the same synergic principles of toxicology. It does not seem to work with everybody — both Susan and I have tried the combination without any interesting results. The city mushroom hunter may find the cool, sweetly scented brackets of that gastronomic joy, the Oyster mushroom (*Plurotus*), its color and size varying with whichever hardwood tree or stump is its host. The variety that grows on dead poplar here is mainly pure white, and is conspicuous enough to be seen from a car when driving along country roads. I have seen the brown variety in the elms around the high school here. Sometimes we sit on top of a hill in the country, and spot our oyster supper with field glasses. A small monkey would be invaluable to run up the trunk of the tree and throw them down like coconuts, for the fairest and the best, as with apples, are always at the top. One find of these shelving, scallop-shaped delicacies is enough for a meal, and they are heavenly, cut up into oyster-sized pieces and fried, with or without egg-and-breadcrumbs first. Then there are delicious *Russulae*, some nutty and crisp, some sweet and soft; and one, my favorite, that tastes of cooked lobster. *Russulae* are excellent for the novice to experiment with: an infinitesimal unswallowed nibble of the raw mushroom gives an immediate clue: the inedible specimens are hotter than pepper. Then there is the wide taste and consistency range of the "Sponge" mushrooms — so called because the undersurface has tubes instead of gills, and looks very like a fine sponge. The *Boletus* was so widely esteemed and used in Ancient Rome that it became almost a synonym for a mushroom; it appears as such in odes; and even the special serving dishes for mushrooms were called *boletarii*. I offer this snippet of historical information because recently I was interested to see that the contents depicted on a packet of dehydrated mushroom soup were unmistakably of the *Boletus* family. I have mentioned some of the obvious and easily distinguished mushrooms, with, to me, interesting tastes, but anyone with an eye perceptive enough to distinguish a dandelion from a daisy, the ability to read (and follow) an elementary textbook, and, above all, the commonsense to try no more than a mouthful of anything new, can develop an individual list of epicurean delights — and benefit from the most peaceful occupation in the world while doing so.

Since the world began we have been "children of light," dependent upon the sun, perishing without: the mushroom has no need of it, and flourishes in darkness. It is small wonder, then, that our earliest ancestors associated the mysteriously growing little children of darkness with all the superstition and fear accorded to creatures and things of night, leaving their doubts in our minds to this day. The strange thing is that in "this day" of nuclear fission and space travel, many questions on the origin and meaning of a fungus still remain a scientific mystery, and its potential in the world of medicine is like a vast untapped mine. As my acquaintance increases I become more and more its devoted admirer: it is a small self-sufficient miracle of the most tranquil dignity, and, unlike all other living growing miracles of nature, it has the quality of utter stillness. Its coloring can be brighter than the most vivid flower, its quieter subtleties of shading surpass any flower; the infinitesimal structural details are unequaled in their exquisite minutiae. It is impossible to know them and to wander in their environment, through woods and pastureland, without the pace of the mind slowing down to their enduring serenity; and when the mind relaxes the eyes and ears gain a new awareness of the microscopic detail of other small miracles — mosses, ferns and wildflowers suddenly stand out in sharper focus than one has ever known; birds, too, for they seem to accept one's slow pace and lack of abrupt movement. Some birds, particularly the inquisitive jays and the chickadees, display an unusually close interest in one's finds. Once, when I was sitting with my back to a log in a newly felled clearing, a hummingbird hovered for nearly a full minute less than five inches from my eyes. Squirrels and chipmunks too are very interested — perhaps because they are jealous of the intrusion into their larders: their teeth marks are on many of the specimens, and often one comes across the evidence of an interrupted meal on a tree stump, or even high up in the branches. One spring I picked mushrooms within three feet of a partridge sitting on her nest, cleverly camouflaged against the dead leaves and a rocky background: I suddenly looked up and found I was staring straight into her eyes — she managed to make them quite blank and expressionless.

Nearly all the well-known native mushrooms have folk names, but these, of course, vary from country to country, and it is best to learn to refer to them by their Latin family names. They each have two: first the family, then the descriptive. This scientific identification becomes then a *lingua franca* that enables one to hunt in any country, and with almost any textbook. There is no more acceptable guise abroad than that of the mushroom hunter (fishing enthusiasts come close), for the basket seems to act as a kind of international passport to wander peacefully through the countryside without attracting any of the attention normally accorded to strangers or tourists. Furthermore, one cannot so decimate or despoil another's countryside, for mushrooms cannot be picked out of existence, like flowers, but will reappear century after century in the same place. Even without leaving this country it can be a most cosmopolitan sport, for every New Canadian represents a nationality with its own specific favorites. I am always astonished how many of these are anathema to another. Sometimes we hunt in Boulevard Park, on the city limits, in the spring or fall, and there we compare our finds with other mushroomers; they can be spotted at once by the basket, and the apparently aimless, meandering type of walk, with head bent, as though deep in thought; or else they are crouched covertly with busy knife. Sometimes they are very recently arrived from their old country, but language is no barrier as we paw through one another's baskets — violent head-shakings or delighted smiles, eyebrows waggling like semaphore flags or greedy smackings of the lips are just as effective. Sometimes we find their baskets filled with mushrooms described as inedible or poisonous in our books; and sometimes they register horror at some of our culinary treasures — often mushrooms that we have eaten with gusto for years. Our friend Mrs. Harmatiuk, who farms near the lake where we have our summer cottages, is from the Ukraine, and the Ukrainians are born mushroomers; yet Mrs. Harmatiuk is convinced that she will find us rolling in agony one day after a puffball feast. And to our certain knowledge she and all her family eat the *Gyrometra esculenta*, the false morel, that is never labeled as anything other than poisonous in the textbooks (mostly because it has an inexplicable selectivity in its victims), and a type of *Lactarius*, or milk mushroom, that is generally considered completely inedible, and upsetting to say the least of it. Similarly the Finnish nationalities will collect one kind that makes the Italians throw up their hands in horror, and vice versa. Susan and I benefit from this pool of international prejudice and eat impartially, the United Nations way.

Textbooks follow this international tendency too, sometimes. We have between us about eight reference books on edible fungi that we regularly use for identification — or for escapist winter reading; the ones with color photographic reproductions are a joy when the snow is several feet deep and the thermometer several inches below zero. One of the best is *Mushrooms of Canada*, published by the Queen's Printer, beautifully illustrated with colored photographs, and plenty of good, solid meat in the descriptions; then we have a selection of English and American works, and Czechoslovakia, Danish and Dutch translations. The difference in national temperament of the authors, and therefore presentations, can be quite amusing, ranging from the impassive restraint of the British to the trails of exclamation marks and excited heavy print of the Czechoslovakians, the pedantic yet indulgent approach of the Canadians ("This is reported to be poisonous, children; however, you are all old enough now to make up your minds about it for yourself"); or the occasional verve but cautionary enthusiasm of the Americans. *Lactarius rufus*, a very common milk mushroom on this continent, is a wonderful example of these variations — I have just picked it out at random from one book, then looked it up in several others — and the descriptions of the taste run from the noncommittal "not pleasant-tasting" of the British to the "excruciatingly acid" of the Americans. All nations are united in condemning it either as inedible or else frankly poisonous — all except Czechoslovakia, and here we learn that it is sold in the open market, and is prized for its ability to flourish in dry weather when there is nothing else available. All it needs is a little more care and trouble in the preparations, says the author; and, as he very reasonably points out, surely this is worth it rather than suffer total mushroom-deprivation. . . .

These varying classifications of "poisonous" and "inedible" need more clarification sometimes, and an open mind and a few grains of salt are helpful to the more experienced. "Poisonous" can vary in its effects from a mild allergy or indigestion to intense intestinal distress; "inedible" can mean that no one has tried boiling it first, then draining it before preparation. But, unless the eater is in such poor health anyway that a mild gastroenteritis could provide just that little extra to upset the balance, *there is only one family of mushrooms that contains a fatally poisonous member*. This is the *Amanita* family, and while it contains many edible and excellent mushrooms (including the Imperial mushroom of ancient Rome — the Caesaria, or *Cibus Deorum*, food of the gods, as it was known), it also contains the fatal Destroying Angel, *Amanita virosa*, and her wicked (though not deadly) sisters, *verna*, *pantherina*, and dubious *umbrina*. I think, then, that there is one simple rule for the amateur: learn to recognize the *Amanita* family backwards and forwards, then avoid them like the plague. Even if you yearn to try the food of the gods, the gastronomic status is hardly worth it if a mistake could transport you painfully and precipitately into their eternal company. And the unappetizing fact that your last mortal meal could easily have been compounded of the brains of seven rabbits and the stomachs of three, chopped up and eaten in raw pellets, should act as a further deterrent. This is as far as science has advanced in its search for an antidote, and the results are as discouraging as the recipe. Poor Claudius died in a protracted agony after his wife Agrippina popped some *Amanitae* into a dish of his favorite mushrooms, so that she could secure the succession for her son, Nero. This regrettable display of maternal aggressiveness, and her abuse of a plate of good mushrooms, brought about its own just deserts, however: the young Emperor soon grew tired of his overbearing busybody of a mother and had her quietly assassinated. The moral for us is — have nothing whatsoever to do with the *Amanitae*.

There is one *Amanita*, however, that deserves more specific mention, for sooner or later the amateur mushroom hunter will read about its propensities, or meet someone who says they know how to prepare it to enjoy these propensities without any unpleasant effects. This is the Fly Agaric, or *A. muscaria*, which looks exactly like a nursery toadstool. It contains, among other substances, mycoatropine, which acts as a brain irritant and produces a state resembling alcoholic intoxication, with a feeling of extraordinary strength and well-being, and sometimes accompanying hallucinations of grandeur and power. The achievement of such an almighty jag, and all for free, holds great appeal for some people. The peasants of a district in northeastern Silesia are reported to celebrate this economical way, and some say the Laplanders know how to make a brew from it with the same results. However, the intoxication can have the wildest, most savage effect on some people apparently; so if anyone should happen to do a good turn to a Silesian or Laplander, then later have him confide the recipe on his last grateful, but expiring, breath, like the Worcestershire Nobleman to his Faithful Butler, I think it would be wiser to thank him gracefully, then forget it forever. If tempted to experiment, one can sprinkle sugar on the enigmatic Fly Cap and watch it lure flies to their paralytically carefree death.

I do not think even that mighty mushroomer Mc-

Ilvaine tried the Fly Cap, and he, as A. H. Smith says in his excellent *Field Guide*, "had more firsthand knowledge of edible native mushrooms than any other person of his day or since, and an enthusiasm that knew no restrictions." Charles McIlvaine was an American, and he wrote a book called *One Thousand American Fungi*. I have not been able to find a copy and only know it from tantalizing fragments quoted in other books. His enthusiasm is most catching, his appetite for edible fungi insatiable, his digestion apparently equine: he was the most intrepid gastronomic explorer of this century, and Smith's field book is dotted with his opinions: "McIlvaine thought highly of it," or he "considered that it made a choice pickle"; "Edible when one is hungry or cannot get better," he says wistfully, or "good as an absorbent, or in an emergency;" . . . then a flash of delightful domestic aptness: "Old caps have a taste like stale lard." His simple faith in fungi, whether as food divine or a panacea of all ills, shines through the pages like a Jack-o-Lantern (or *Clitocybe illudens*) as he modestly confides that he once "saved the life of a beautiful young lady by feeding her Champignons when she was unable to keep anything else down." I never read these immortal words without thinking of the operatic finale that Puccini could have made of them.

McIlvaine's book was published in 1900, and I can only suppose that he is no longer with us; and hope that his ambrosia is indeed compounded of mushrooms (as Robert Graves would have us believe from his recent ingenuous theory), freshly gathered from the Elysian Fields, and eaten in the company of the illustrious fungi fanatics who preceded him: Plutarch and Hippocrates, who used them in his pharmaco-poeia; Pliny, Martial, and Juvenal, who wrote that it was easier to turn down material riches than a plate of mushrooms; and Theophrastus, who antedated Mc-Ilvaine's authorship by about two thousand years; and, of course, poor old short-changed Claudius, and many, many more.

Most people think of the late summer or fall as a time to go a-mushrooming, and certainly they are most abundant in the fall — last year, after a three-year absence, the popular Honey Mushroom (*Armillaria mellea*) reappeared, for some cyclic reason, in such abundance that it seemed that every fallen log or stump in the bush was covered with dense frills; these are the mushrooms that bring normally non-enthusiastic hunters out in their thousands in September; they keep very well when boiled for some time, then frozen. (Some people are allergic to them.) Mrs. Harmatiuk, our Ukrainian friend, sautés them, after boiling, with onions, then covers them in dollops of sour cream. But there is really nothing to compare with the fresh, cool delicacy of the spring mushrooms: the fragrant Oysters, or the apricot-smelling Chanterelles, like bright yellow trumpets springing from last year's dead leaves, needles and bracken. Perhaps it is because we wait so long for them they are so particularly delicious in our spring.

As I write this, surrounded by mouth-watering textbooks, it is early March, and the snow is still piled in high drifts; there is, it is true, an unmistakable warmth in the sun, but I have plenty of time to think about spring, or what passes for spring, in May. I hardly know which spring treat I look forward to most: that long-awaited day when the snow has retreated so that one may walk through the forests again, unencumbered by heavy clothing, snowshoes or skis, and walk for the sheer joy of it; the spring ecstasy of birds in trees that soar in an almost ecclesiastic beauty, the pure lines of the branches as yet unblurred by leaves still captive in the swollen buds; the silver myriads of smelt battling the jubilant spring torrents; the delicious secret of the tightly rolled fiddlehead ferns — the only word that I can think of to describe their taste is "innocent" — or succulent young bulrush heads; or, and now I think I come to the heart of the matter, the morels. . . .

Morels are the forerunners of the season's edible fungi, and they rise, cool and delicate, from an earth still deeply frostbound, sometimes skirting the edges of snowdrifts; their heads, conical or oval, are like smooth sponges, exquisitely wrought in deep intricate patterns of pits, blending in all shades of honey against the damp, fallen-leaf mosaic on the floor of the forest, or shaming the winter's dead grasses in clearings.

Finding morels in quantity brings the same emotions to a mushroomer as gold to a prospector, and anyone who confides the location of his own private morel factory is a friend indeed.

Susan and I searched for three years before we found any, for there is an element of time and weather conditions in their appearance, and their season lasts only about a week or ten days here. I have never forgotten our first sight of them — halfway up the side of one of the "Nor'westers," part of the pre-Cambrian range that extends along the southwest, in the last week of May when the hillsides were still running with little snow-creeks. We searched there because we had noticed a lot of rough-barked black poplar among the more usual mixed stands of aspen, birch and spruce, and we knew that morels liked black poplar. We had searched apart that morning, covering a large area, and had just met, thoroughly discouraged, when, "Those bears were here not very long ago," said Susan, staring down at the indisputably recent evidence, and we decided to move off elsewhere, for Raimie was the only dog with us, and if we wanted to share his protectorate we would have to stay together; neither of us having any desire to get between a sow bear and her cubs perhaps — she is inclined to be irritable in the spring, and has an exaggerated sense of her maternal duties. Then, "Look," Susan said — and there, just a few feet away, was our first morel; and as our eyes became ac-

customed enough to their shape to isolate them from
the camouflaging background of brown leaves and
mosses, we saw that the ground was covered with a
little brown regiment of them. The Koh-i-noor Dia-
mond and the Northwest Passage were paltry discoveries in comparison to this: whole platoons of
bears could have marched by and we would not
have noticed them. Even to write about it makes me
yearn. This year I am going to try them stuffed:
I read a most savory-sounding recipe in Sylvia Boor-
man's delightful book *Wild Plums and Brandy* just
last week.

As I am assuming an adherence to the textbooks,
and a normal quota of common sense, I have only one
warning (apart from the *Amanitas*) for anyone who is
thinking of taking up the ancient sport of mushroom
hunting: you will bore your friends to tears with
your enthusiasms. They will cast a lackluster eye on
your most cherished specimens; and they will tend
to melt into the countryside whenever they see you
coming with a filled basket. They will consider it a
miracle that you continue to survive from meal to
meal, yet they will endlessly repeat the remarkably
dangerous folklore that toadstools are terrible, bad
mushrooms tarnish silver, good mushrooms peel . . .
(It will be useless to point out that toadstools and
mushrooms are one and the same, that some of the
pleasantest tarnish silver, and that the Destroying
Angel peels beautifully.) They will tell you, too, of

poor Great-aunt Kate, who died so suddenly (and just two days before her ninety-first birthday) and had *eaten some mushrooms that day*. Or misguided Cousin Henry, who consumed, on the banks of the Amazon, what he *thought* was *Agaricus sylvestris*, and was very shortly afterwards consumed in turn by crocodiles. Or . . . but almost certainly you will collect your own rare specimens of equally doomed relatives along with your mushrooms.

Sometimes, however, I think I sense a covert envy when they come upon us after a peaceful summer afternoon spent in the bush: Susan and I reclining comfortably on either side of an electric frying pan, a tall, clinking glass in one hand, a fork in the other. In the frying pan exciting little groups of different mushrooms sauté gently in butter, the pepper and salt is handy: we are about to spear our catch with our forks, then later cast our vote for the Mushroom of the Day. On every surface around us are new, as yet unidentified specimens, resting on their gills on scraps of paper under glass, making spore prints for us. . . . And as we sit there, infinitely replete and content, various small minions appear from surrounding cottages with the offerings they have picked for us — for some quite small children have learned to recognize quite a few species. We hope we are training a new, strong, fit generation for future mushroom hunting.

Confessions of a Noisemaker

I AM inhibited in any public noisemaking by the thought of listening ears, and as there are few places left in this shrinking world without them, I remained, until I went out West to hunt ducks, a stopped-up vehicle with two decades of incipient noise within me. In northern Manitoba and Saskatchewan the world seems vast and untenanted, and beyond the last strip of farmland, stretching to the Arctic, lies the endless, earless tundra. . . .

Year after year we come, and I have always hunted with the same tolerant companions; having proved over the years that I will not incommode them by getting lost, injured, or strung up on a barbed wire fence, and that I will arrive back at a given time and a given place with all my wits and belongings about me, I am free to wander at will and no questions asked. I stuff my pockets with shells, hack off a piece of sausage in case I am overcome with hunger, then into my game pocket go Myrtle and Byrtle, Maud and Martin, four collapsible rubber decoys. Sometimes I take a tire repair kit, for one of these days

I mean to repair the rent in poor Maud's bottom so that she may ride the water as buoyantly as her companions instead of sagging weakly over a supporting branch. As a last gesture I take my gun. There is a delicious feeling of vice about to be indulged as Raimie and I wander off across the rolling fields. It is the time of day, from noon until about three o'clock, when there is little activity in the skies, and consequently none among my companions, who are sleeping off their lunch in haystacks, or in the long soft grass at the edge of the bluffs.

I find a slough, half a mile or more away, preferably with a screen of stunted poplar and alder, and in a sound-proofing dip. I launch Myrtle and Byrtle and Martin, and they swing demurely at their anchoring cords, beaks into the wind. Poor Maud flops over a tuft in the shallows, but I am unmoved. We find some cover; usually the reeds and grasses are so high by the slough edges that I only have to sit down to disappear. Officially I am now a keen wildfowler, shaming the sloth of my companions, sitting watchfully over my decoys in the hope of a shot. Unofficially, I am about to make the welkin ring.

I like to be fashionable and think it had its origins in childhood: as children we were required to perform, vocally or upon the piano, for the entertainment of parental guests. These were Command Performances in the purest sense, for it was a brave child indeed who displayed any reluctance or what was called "gaucherie" (a useful parental category covering almost everything): he received what we called "The Look" — a piercing glance of such meaningful wait-till-later compulsion that it paralyzed rebellion in the bud, and activated an almost immediate musical response. The Look also paralyzed all future hope of public performances, as I found out later when emancipated from it — without its powerful catalyst I was mute and useless with inhibited embarrassment. This lack was no loss to the world (a gain if anything), and certainly no serious inconvenience to me — until that fateful day when I heard someone "calling" ducks for the first time out hunting: "Mack, mack, mack," he quacked without apparent effort, and the mallards answered, turned and came over. There was quite a variation in calls: the Highball, the Lonesome Hen, the Surprise Recognition, the Feeding Call, etc. In the depths of my long-silent soul a deep yearning was born: I longed, as I had never longed before, to do the same. It looked so easy; I felt so in tune that it seemed I only had to open my mouth for similar true and beautiful quacks to ring out; but every time I tried nothing emerged from my frozen lips but faint embarrassed squeaks.

Then one day I was lying on my back beside a little slough, half asleep in the noonday sun, a safe half-section removed from my companions' ears. A raven passed overhead, and cawed. Unbidden, effortless, up from the depths of my soul and out through my mouth emerged and soared through the skies a hoarse raucous reply of such apparent accuracy and import that the raven, after a surprised glance behind, lowered his altitude by several feet and inquired where I was. "Here," I croaked harshly. "Where?" cawed the bird, puzzled, but still losing height. I beamed him in like a control tower, emitting encouraging directional croaks, but just when it looked as though he were making a last turn over the runway before coming in for a landing, Raimie suddenly sat up and ruined everything. The raven, a poor mixed-up bird by now, flew off indignantly — and with him went the cork of my years of bottled-up noisemaking: I spent the rest of the afternoon happily confusing the local raven population. The only drawback was that I could only croak in a horizontal position, and even to this day I have never achieved upright mastery.

Success followed success in the days that remained; whenever possible I would gather up my rubber quartette, my dog, the garlic sausage and my gun, and depart in the direction of the nearest slough out of earshot. I became a moderate magpie, a piercingly accurate jay, and a fair snipe. Emancipated by this mastery I sang rollicking sea shanties to the sympathetic vastness of the empty prairie horizons, and practiced whistling through my teeth; Mimi expired from her couch among the bulrushes, and Butterfly parted from her Pinkerton, their last sobbing notes swallowed up in the boundless tundra; I even yodeled. Raimie accepted all this with his usual tolerant calm, and the only time he appeared to be at all uneasy was when I branched out into a Santa Claus ho-ho-hoing.

There is no knowing how far I might have got in that first triumphant year: the return to civilization dammed my outpourings effectively. I had thought that I might keep up my repertoire, possibly in the garage or basement; but inhibitions must be governed by some common level, like a spring within: no sooner does one rid oneself of one set than another wells up to take its place. It seemed now that I was unable to emote without Myrtle, Byrtle, Maud and Martin, gun, dog and sausage. I tried setting them all out one day in the basement when there was no one at home, but it was a total failure: no sound was forthcoming, and even my teeth refused to be whistled through; the silence and loneliness of the West was apparently essential as well. For eleven and a half months, magpies, ravens, peewits, Butterflies, Mimis and Santa Claus seethed and boiled within me, waiting for the release of the next October's hunting trip.

This was the year that the geese were so plentiful, thousands upon thousands, yelping and baying in the skies, honking, gabbling and gossiping in the stubble fields. Four days of unsuccessful attempts to join in reduced my voice to a whisper, and Throte Eze pastilles became a staple in my diet. Not that the days were entirely without reward, however, for out of my abortive honkings emerged quite unexpectedly one day the unmistakable bark of a performing seal; and, less exotic but equally gratuitous, the muffled coughing of a mule deer in a thicket. But this was poor consolation at the time, for I longed only to win vocal recognition from that exclusive airborne choir, and have it veer majestically from its course in answer to my earthbound honking. I had no ulterior motive either, for I was armed only with a camera. At last, listening one morning to the tantalizing clamor overhead, I realized what was wrong: I had tried to be a *chorus* of geese. I had been attempting something like singing all four parts of a quartette simultaneously. Now I listened carefully and isolated a contralto of about my range in the flock, who kept up an obliging steady honking. I threw back my head, to make my neck as long and gooselike as possible, opened my throat as though I were about to pour something down it, then fooled it at the last moment by howling like a lovelorn wolf — and out came a perfect yelping honk. My contralto friend answered, an echelon of her relatives joined in, and so did the dog; and as I crouched there, howling my heart out, wingless but ecstatic, the long V wavered and turned; and our unlovely duet rose and mingled at last with the wild harmony above as they flew directly over us.

Now there was no holding me, and anything that flew or walked in Saskatchewan was grist to my noise mill. Soon I could discomfort a squirrel with a return volley of its own fishwife scolding; by making a noise like a soprano tigress purring in a filing cabinet I could bring the bluebills dipsy-doodling overhead. In quieter mood I was a grasshopper clicking in the grass, or a creaking tree. But all in private, all for my mute audience of Myrtle, Byrtle, Maud and Martin. And still I could not be a mallard: as a likely Lonesome Hen I went unheeded, my Highball Call drew nothing but derisive quacks; and whatever I was saying in the guttural Dugaw-dugaw-dugaws of my Feeding Call must have been very rude indeed, for one and all the ducks would jump about five feet and accelerate madly out of range, quacking like indignant old maids. It was very discouraging.

One year, in desperation, I bought a duck call, a little wooden instrument, made by the gnarled old hands of craftsmen steeped in wildfowl lore, so the directions said, and went on to say, "With the lips pursed around the mouthpiece take a deep breath from the stomach and expel it slowly, at the same time saying 'Hoot, hoot, hoot.' Proper breathing," it added, "is apparent when the Adam's apple moves slightly up and down. . . ." It is not easy to transfer a lifetime habit of breathing from the lungs to the stomach, and I lacked an Adam's apple, nevertheless I persevered and blew gamely on. The only bird that appeared in answer to my agonized hootings was an enormous snowy owl who perched on a nearby rat house and so unnerved me with its unwinking saucer-eyed stare that I prepared to gather up Martin and the Girls and decamp.

Winding in the little lead anchors of four apparently plump ducks, squashing them into shapeless little rubber parcels tied around with cord, under the close incredulous censorship of a large snowy owl is a nerve-wracking experience: clumsy at the best of times in heavy thigh boots, I now became positively catatonic. One boot stuck in the glutinous marsh mud and I hopped and teetered wildly on one leg; shells, sausage, and the duck call rained out of my pockets when I bent to heave on the boot. I think it was the utter silence of my audience that destroyed my morale in the end. I tried to break it with a nonchalant "Well, hi, there — " but even to my ears the note of camaraderie rang about as true as a tin dime: the unblinking saucer eyes seemed to snap even wider open, and the long Presbyterian beak settle more disapprovingly. Maud, the last to be picked up, had two Band-Aids crossed over the rent in her bottom, and now, at the thought of those critical eyes riveted on my slovenly handiwork, my last shred of confidence went. . . .

I never went back to retrieve the duck call. Wild horses could not have dragged me there. I became resigned to the fact that I was never going to establish any rapport with mallards. But it seemed a pity not to use my new-found faculty of stomach breathing: I would master a woodwind instrument in the solitudes. It would be something small and simple that could be concealed in the pocket of my hunting jacket. I found a thing like a baby flute, called a Flutophone, in the toy department at Christmastime, and during the long silent months before the next hunting season I built up an idyllic picture of myself, Pan-like among the bulrushes, while all around the little wild furry things crept out of their burrows to listen. . . .

It was a dismal failure; instead of our normally moderately warm October, it was bitterly cold with snow flurries; and the only time I was able to wander far enough away from the others to indulge myself in my secret vice, all the smaller furry animals had very sensibly holed up snugly somewhere. Instead there appeared, summoned by the cold quavery notes of "There is a happy land," a horde of mammoth cattle, led by a snorting creature with mighty horns who looked big enough to be extinct, when silhouetted against a lowering sky on the crest of the rise above me. Behind me where I crouched, as scheduled, among the bulrushes lay the quagmire shores of a small slough; above and before were the massed ranks of my audience, the frosty vapor of their breath swirling and eddying in clouds from which their horned heads and rolling eyes slowly materialized and vanished, only to appear again. It looked like some horrible mythological mix-up: the Minotaur leading a squadron of the Valkyrie down the cloud-wreathed slopes of Olympus.

Raimie apparently decided that it was all so preposterous that he would have no part in it, for he faded quietly into the bulrushes behind, leaving me to deal with the situation. I do not care for bulls. This monster pawed the ground with its hoof like an impatient conductor, and I stared at him, paralyzed in mind and body: there was something familiar about its expression. . . . It was The Look. "Play — " it said quite clearly, "play — or else . . ." My obedient reaction did my early training credit: the Flutophone snapped to my lips and I played. Never has "There is a happy land" been performed with such moving eloquence or intensity of feeling; it would have brought my parents' guests to their feet with a storm of applause and bravos. This present audience was so moved that it drew ten feet closer, and I only halted them by emptying my lungs in a sustained panic-stricken blast on one note. On and on I blew that frigid afternoon, keeping them at bay with steady foghorn blasts; any variation on this theme, any attempt at a tune or a scale to keep the circulation going in my numbed fingers, produced such a surging response that I thought for a moment of luring them, like the children of Hamelin, across the countryside, walking backwards until I felt the first reassuring jag of barbed wire — until I remembered that the tenth backward step would be into the marsh. A pause for breath brought an ominous unease of massive hooves shifting impatiently and the rumblings of many stomachs. I bleated despairingly on, so cold that snowflakes no longer thawed on my puffing cheeks, until at last I blew myself into a vacuum of uncaring euphoria: I would not wait for my audience to charge me — I would charge *them*; waving and shouting, hurling my Flutophone into their midst, I would come at them; and if I could reach my gun in time, and my paralyzed fingers were still capable of operating it, I would launch my surprise assault with a threatening salvo or two. I stood up to try. But one leg had gone to sleep under me and I lurched over; with a snort of pure terror, his eyes rolling wildly, the bull backed up the hillside, then wheeled, revealing a conspicuous matronly udder, and charged through the ranks behind, and the herd stampeded after. As the thunder of the galloping, panic-stricken hooves died away, my noble dog emerged from the bulrushes and barked twice. I caught his eye, and he had the grace to look embarrassed. I kept very quiet about the whole affair myself.

A good many years have passed since the raven first flew off with the cork on my stoppered noise-making, and time has left its mark upon our little company. Martin and Les Girls have lost the bloom of youth and are weathered to a uniform gray; every year they lose a little more buoyancy, and so do

Raimie and I; poor gallant Maud still collapses without her crutches; only the garlic sausage comes fresh upon the annual scene. And — shiny and new, pristine bright, still wrapped in its tissue paper, awaiting the October moment — a dear little harmonica this year.

Time Out of Mind

Now that it has ebbed, I realize that the tide in my affairs that washed me up on the shores of archaeology-cum-anthropology, and left me stranded on a Pleistocene beach like some bewildered prehistoric whale, was undoubtedly the same predestined force that regularly wrecked my schooner on the jagged outer reefs, then washed me over the coral strand and into the lagoons of my childhood desert islands. . . .

When the storm had abated, and the castaways took stock of their plight, the classic beginning to every second chapter, their ensuing ingenuity and ability to carve out a workable rudimentary civilization from the materials to hand always fascinated me as a child. The first story I ever remember having read to me was *Robinson Crusoe*, and later I read and re-read it myself, starting again at the beginning the moment it was finished, just like painting the Forth bridge. *The Swiss Family Robinson* was even better; not the shortened version so often found today but a wonderfully fat volume, profusely illustrated and

complete in every last moralization (and every grue-
some detail of poor Grizzle's demise in the folds of
the boa constrictor and subsequent mastication; five
hours from ear to hoof — Papa Robinson timed it;
children were apparently credited with stronger stomachs in those days) and its pages crammed with
useful tidbits of information on how to improve one's
lot and live more graciously on desert islands. I used
to spend hours daydreaming of starting from scratch
on my island utopia and putting all this practical information to the test. Thanks to Mr. Robinson, that
bottomless well of How To Do It lore, I knew how
to make a Unique Machine for boiling whale blubber;
I could construct a sun or sand clock, train ostriches,
open oysters and manufacture sago; if a sturgeon had
been caught in my coconut fiber fishnet I knew just
how to make isinglass windows from its bladder. I
could even — and as I write I feel the urge to do so
— make waterproof boots (beloved, familiar gumboots), with a clay mold, taken from my sand-filled
socks, then painted over with layers of latex tapped
from the nearest rubber tree. It would have been a
luckless Man Friday who made his imprint on my
solitary sands, for I would have been a fearful bore
to live with: like Papa Robinson, one innocent question would have released a pedantic torrent of information.

This childhood preoccupation with carving out an
existence by my own unaided efforts used to end,

invariably, I remember, with that baffled, mind-boggling feeling that used to overcome me — and still does — when staring up at a cloudless blue sky and trying to make my small limited mind grasp that the blue is a void, endless infinity, *nothing*, not even omega. For, sooner or later, a fearful, nagging doubt insinuated itself into every castaway installment of my self-told story: *What if one did not have a knife, or a goat, or a gun to start with?* Or, worse still, had not read *Swiss Family Robinson?* How on earth did one go about forging steel for that most necessary knife (what, for that matter, *was* steel?), substitute for a goat, manufacture a gun, or *any* kind of weapon? The childhood mind always retreated tiredly, as from the sky, and thought it would think about it some other time: tomorrow it would look up steel in the encyclopedia, tomorrow. . . . Then "tomorrow," I suppose, became the day when school life took its inexorable mundane hold upon me, and all my dreams and hopes of putting my knowledge to the test sank under the weight of irregular verbs and average mean rainfalls, to be dredged up occasionally throughout the years and used in general knowledge tests, or essays.

Until last year, when they suddenly floated up from the depths of my subconscious, like *Coelacanthus*, the four-legged fish who was thought to be extinct until he suddenly appeared in someone's fish-net. And if the simile seems unnecessarily abstruse, it also points quite clearly the state of my mind, for I had become involved in a parallel of island survival, only this time it was evolutionary: collecting, categorizing and later reading about vast numbers of Stone Age artifacts: hand axes, points, blades, scrapers and burins by the hundreds, although it was sometime before I recognized the parallel.

The area of this archaeological find is enormous — to be thought of in terms of miles rather than the more usual yards — and is probably the manufacturing or workshop site of a people who lived by hunting along the shores of what was then a Pleistocene lake, anything from nine thousand to three thousand years before Lake Superior dropped to its present level over two hundred feet below. Of course only the rank amateur ever feels qualified to make such unguarded statements: professional archaeologists and anthropologists are, and with good reason, a cagey race; let them come out on a rash definitive limb about anything, and somewhere, someone else will hook a coelacanth or dig up a saber-toothed tiger from a peat bog, where it had no chronological right to be, with a hideously wrong type of spearpoint (culturally wrong) between its ribs, and upset the whole theory by a millennium or two.

The small but very important Brohm Site which was excavated here a dozen years ago is a good example of the exciting lucky dip element in North American archaeology, for some of the weapon points found here were the Plainview and Eden Valley type of points found in Texas and Wyoming, and were able to be dated by the Carbon 14 test, as they were found in conjunction with the skeletons of animals: the animals were mostly long since extinct, and the approximate carbon date was between six and seven thousand years ago. Yet it seems to have been generally considered that as far north as this the ice cap would not have retreated sufficiently for the establishment of the plant life necessary to support browsing animals — and, of course, hard on the heels of the animals, Man came panting over the anthropological horizon.

The Brohm Site was a small one and its findings relatively few; but any thoughts that the Brohm People were a small but adventurous advance guard of the Pleistocene Pioneers, hopefully camped on a glacier, waiting for a nice sunny day to melt it and bring hordes of mastodon galloping over the instant vegetation, should be dispelled by the discovery of our huge manufacturing site: on the same postglacial beach level and apparently of the same period or periods of culture as we, too, found Plainview and Eden points. In fact, judging by the masses of evidence that he left behind, finished, half finished, broken, or discarded at a fault in the stone, the piles of chips and fragments of his handiwork, Man was obviously having a high old time here, with game in abundance, when by geographical rights his appearance was premature by several thousand years.

All this I state from away out on the precarious outermost end of my ignorant limb, yet blithely confident that I will not be shot down in flames by the professionals in their field, for a target of such reckless naïeveté would surely not be worth the leveling of their sights. It is a very happy position. And anyway, the professionals, when they come to correlate the evidence this year, should have a high old time themselves with the masses of unexcavated material waiting to see the scientific light of day on our site. But there is one thing that I am completely certain about: not one of them will ever have a closer understanding of old time, live with it so intimately, or make such interesting unscientific discoveries about it as I did last year. . . .

At the time when a friend, Hugh Cummins, found this site, I was unconcerned with this or for that matter any archaeology; and as for anthropology I had seldom given a thought, beyond enjoying the Flintstones, to the intellectual gap between my cave-dwelling ancestors and the astronauts of today. But Hugh is a most enthusiastic and interesting man on his favorite subject, and one day he very generously included me in the extremely small group of people who knew the secret location of his new-found site, and invited me to help. He had been searching for such a place for years, convinced that it must exist where massive outcroppings of jasper were to be found in close conjunction with the ancient beaches formed as the glaciers retreated, but looking for such a place over even a comparatively restricted length of shoreline is a Herculean, lifetime task, unless one is lucky enough to have an observant farmer who will recognize an artifact for what it is when plowing his fields, as happened at the Brohm Site. One day, when Hugh was exploring some country in company with the twin sons of a local farmer, they picked up a perfect point, but only one; ". . . However, as the boys appeared interested, I described to them the type of location I sought. . . . Eventually we came to a quarry, the hill above which seemed to meet with all my requirements. . . . The northern approach up which we walked was a long gradual incline with low gravel and shale ridges caused by bulldozers having pushed material down the slope to the quarry below. On this hill, within an hour, we picked up some twenty artifacts; flakes and fragments of jasper were apparent everywhere. . . ."

On this hill, and the surrounding area, within the next few weeks, I picked up some two or three hundred artifacts; flakes and fragments of jasper later became apparent everywhere around me as I passed some two or three thousand centuries. . . .

The site was a paradise for amateur archaeologists, for the area was honeycombed with quarries, down the steep sandy sides of which the artifacts had rained

out from the darker humus level at the top, like cur-
rants out of a fruit cake, when the land was sliced
through. Bulldozers had obligingly scraped off the
humus to gravel or rock level on the hill surfaces,
churning up little treasure troves of well-stocked
ridges, or exposing artifacts peeping coyly out of the
gravel; even the bulldozed trees held excitement
among their exposed roots, some of my best specimens being plucked like blueberries from the still
adherent soil. I say a paradise for amateurs with purpose, for there is nothing more destructive or in-
furiating to the professional than Sunday afternoon
seekers, who make unscientific excavations, digging
little holes and pulling things out, on the Little Jack
Horner principle; to be of any acceptable value excavations must be painstakingly mapped out, then
worked and sifted stratigraphically, and with a delicate accuracy. (I say this with a certain smug com-
placency, hoping that the professionals will recognize
this sop from an amateur who knows her place —
theoretically anyway.) Here, all we had to do (and
what is more, if we did *not* do it, some new bulldozer might arrive, or gravel truck load up and eventually dump our treasures in a new sewer project)
was to pick up the exposed artifacts, number them by
code with chalk, then mark their location on a survey
map. We were sworn to secrecy, not even telling our
families of the location, as it was obviously important
to keep Rabbit's Friends and Relations from swarm-

ing over the site, and possibly removing something of great importance. In the weeks left to us before the first snowfall, Hugh's plan was to make as large and representative a collection as possible, documented and photographed; then write a full preliminary report in the hopes that this tantalizing bait would lure an official party of excavators out of museum basements and up to Lake Superior in the spring.

Once I had learned to recognize the work of human hands, however crudely executed, and was not to be taken in by likely looking but naturally fractured and water-washed pieces of jasper, quartzite or taconite, I found that the eye responded very quickly to its new knowledge, often picking out the genuine article at some distance, even from among a pile of bulldozed fragments. I became more and more absorbed in my new pastime, driving out and spending hours in and around the quarries armed with my favorite archaeological tool, a two-pronged steel weed extractor with a long wooden handle, and accompanied by Raimie, my *Doppelgänger* dog, who, of all the outdoor pursuits which he and I have enjoyed together over the years, found picking up dull stones the most abysmally boring. Sometimes I scrambled up and down between the quarries; sometimes I sauntered along the beds, plucking scrapers and blades at eye level from the steep sandy sides; and sometimes I wandered along rutted tracks between young jackpines, spotting artifacts in the ruts or the banks at the side; but my most rewarding finds came when I crawled on hands and knees across the hills and ridges, and most of the time I covered the countryside this way. One of us had found a tiny perfect awl, about an inch long, and even though it was like looking for a needle in a haystack on the grand scale, I wanted to find one to match. My slow crawl baffled and frustrated Raimie; he could never make up his mind whether to slither slowly after on his belly, or wait until I had covered ten yards, then drag himself to his feet, pad wearily after, and with much overdone melancholy sink down again. For some reason the place made him uneasy, and he would not leave me for the temporary private explorations which he usually enjoys if I am mush-rooming, for example. I soon learned to avoid his accusing eye by never looking behind me, and the martyred sighs following in my wake sounding like a seal at a blowhole, or sometimes like a soul *in ex-tremis*, soon became nothing more than a peaceful accompaniment to the soughing of the pines.

It was a most glorious fall, a real Indian summer, and a most tranquil occupation; the quarries were deserted, and during most of those still, cloudless golden days the only other sounds accompanying Raimie were the soft hush of sandfalls down the long sloping banks, the rustle of leaves and the whisper-ings of the drying grasses. Later on, flock after flock of geese passed directly overhead, sometimes so high that although I could hear them in the still air I could

barely make out the V's; sometimes low enough for
me to see that there were snow geese among the
Great Canadas, so that the mixed V's looked like
strange checkered boomerangs sailing across the sky.
We saw deer quite often, and once we startled a
young moose and watched him canter off like an un-
gainly colt across a low ridge and into the shelter
of the trees; and many evenings as I worked a particular area until dusk I saw the same big dog fox trot
along his routine evening path — across a wide shallow excavation, then a light jump onto the far bank,
a long pause, looking up at us, then off towards the
sand dunes. These idyllic hours were only interrupted
when the deer season opened and occasional hunters
used the quarries for rifle target practice. Raimie and
I on all fours in our muted and golden browns would
have made an irresistible target for some trigger-happy
hunter, so I unearthed a red cap and jacket, and tied
a red scarf in a voluminous bow around Raimie's neck.
All my ingenuity, which included adhesive tape and
elastic bands, could not keep another red bow on his
provocative tail, which with its almost white undersurface could be mistaken for a deer's scut.

The world, when viewed at a continuous close
level as I crawled happily across it, had a new and
fascinating perspective where pebbles became boul-
ders, little ridges mountains; and for the first time I
saw and isolated the minuscule rainbow colors of
water-washed sand and gravel, smooth and polished

by waves that lapped there thousands of years ago.
I remember suddenly looking up from the ground
one afternoon to a flock of cedar waxwings gossiping in a mountain ash above me, and in the sudden
transition from my Lilliputian world, where ants and
beetles were normal-sized, they looked for a moment
as big as turkey buzzards. There was a strange, other-
world remoteness about this place, a feeling, peaceful
yet definable of presence, that I can only compare
to that experienced once in a remote highland glen —
coming upon the tumbledown outline, almost ob-
scured by bracken, of a croft, and the still falling of
some listening, waiting expectancy all around me.

The enchanted tranquil days slipped by, and I have
never been so content. Now I was taking my lunch
as well, returning only because I could no longer see
in the dusk that comes so swiftly here. Usually when
one is walking, pottering along, or gathering something that requires no mental effort, only observation,
the mind becomes either a delightful vacuum or else
a still pond, its surface rippled only by the occasional
fleeting thought. At first this was the case with me,
but as I returned each evening with bulging pockets
and the piles of jasper multiplied and were laid out
in rows on the ping-pong table in the basement, it
became increasingly easy to understand the uses of
the weapons and implements, and resolve problems of
categorization, and I became completely absorbed,
until one day I realized that the thoughts were no

longer in a vacuum or fleeting but were positively churning up the surface of my mind into whitecaps: the tidal forces were flowing, the past was taking hold of me, and its people were coming into focus. So often one found what seemed to be the exact site where a worker had sat and chipped away at his spearpoint or pick or blade. Once I found a broken blade and later matched it to its missing part on the ping-pong table; another time I found the broken half a few yards away, and could almost hear the grunt of disgust, or prehistoric equivalent of damn, as its maker threw it away. Once I prodded a loose shelf of earth by an overturned tree, and, just as though I had hit the jackpot in a fruit machine, a pile of fragments rained out along with a hammer-stone, two perfect ovoid blades, and one half-finished one: I was curiously touched by the mute eloquence of the little pile at my feet; apart from the light dusting of sand, it was just as though their owner had left them only a few minutes rather than thousands of years ago. I found myself indulging in all sorts of fancies as to why he had never come back: had he spotted some buffalo and rushed off after them, then forgotten where he had been working; had the dusk fallen suddenly as it did for me, and he had crawled out of his cave in the morning to find his site covered with snow; or had someone jealously bopped him on the head with one of those massive worked clunkers of jasper that I often came across, and which would have been heavy enough to make a bronto-saurus stagger in its tracks? It was like some tantaliz-ing half-finished conversation overheard in a bus — one would never know.

I would go home, wash the sand off my day's find, and add them to the collection, then find myself sit-ting in the middle of it, like a broody possessive hen, thinking of ancient Man and his artifacts. I had my favorites by now, some that so exactly fitted my hand, I felt they must have been made by someone the same size; one where the jasper was banded by layers of color, and when I ran my fingers across the edges they felt so finely worked, the surface so smooth and handled, that it seemed whoever had owned this blade had loved it too. Some were exquisitely slender blades, the entire surface covered with the oblique and con-summately executed technique that I had learned to identify as "pressure flaking" . . . or scrapers with such a fine saw edge that it was appreciable only under a magnifying glass; three or four of the treas-ured Plainview points were there, one I dearly loved was so wafer-thin that the gray jaspery taconite felt almost metallic. But the majority of the artifacts were quite startlingly crude by comparison; and still others looked as though they had been executed by a spastic ape in a rough sea. These looked exactly like the illus-trations of the first crude eoliths, the "dawn stones" that the first hairy paw had picked up and banged on a rock in the hope of fracturing it to a more convenient and sharper form for killing or skinning.

I found out, even though the books were so guarded that they hardly said a thing without attaching an escape rider to it, that there were several stages and hundreds of thousands of years between these dawn stones and the beautiful slender refinements resulting from the flint-knapping technique of pressure flaking: The first forward step involved the co-ordination of both hands apparently: banging your stone with another stone so that you chipped off flakes with a definite end in view. Next some primitive perfectionist discovered that if he interposed a pointed stick or bone splinter between the flint and hammerstone he could produce much finer and more controlled results with his chipping. Then came the final step, the important discovery of removing flakes by pressure alone. Someone, Neanderthal Man probably, beneath whose unprepossessing exterior dwelt the soul of a craftsman and a philosopher apparently, noticed that if he just took it easily instead, and pressed slowly, firmly and continuously over the surface of his work, he could control to a miraculous certainty the flaking of the chips. And as Neanderthal Man was probably the first to survive thousands of glacial winters in his cave, he had plenty of time to perfect this technique, and dream up all sorts of nice pattern variations.

All this information only puzzled me more: thousands and thousands of years spanning the gap of achievement from crude hunks of flint to pressure-flaked products meant that our first Cummins Site Man must have been living not just on the fringe but *under* the glacier — not a very practical thing to do really. However, I decided to leave that for the professionals to worry about: picking up artifacts after a bulldozer had scraped the ground clear of soil made it impossible for us to tell whether there had been any accumulative layers between the different types, so it would have to be worried about scientifically (none of the books I read were ever fanciful enough to come up with the suggestion that perhaps Pleistocene Man's skill as a group was not consistent; that perhaps there were the inevitable lower I.Q.'s even then — after all, there must have been a lot of interbreeding — who made the dawn stone type, and the intelligentsia, who worked less hard and produced better results, with pressure). But although I had discarded the local problem I was still left with the general one, that terrible, baffling chronological gap that seemed to have been accepted by everyone else so easily. I brooded and brooded over it; thirty thousand, forty thousand, perhaps even more than fifty thousand years. What on earth had Man been doing with himself all that time? Surely if he had had the intelligence to pick up his stone and bang it he could have progressed just a *little* more rapidly? After all, he had known the properties of fire quite early on; I had seen several pictures of him, undoubtedly simian and beetle-browed, but quite cozy in his cave, a nice fire burning at the entrance. The more I thought about him the more maddeningly retarded he became, and when I read that the wheel was unknown in North America until the coming of the white man I became positively angry and frustrated, with North American Man in particular: surely to goodness he could have thought of a wheel, if he had managed a bow and arrow; a simple old wheel, just the slice off the end of a log, was not asking too much. . . . What *had* he done with himself then, to be in such a suspended state of progress for positively millenniums — and then to accelerate with such hideous speed in the last two centuries? The only possible excuse I could think of was that he might have been irregularly frozen into one of his enigmatic glaciers, like some dormant bacillus or lichen, emerging several thousand years later when they melted sufficiently. This would understandably retard his progress, but I did not think my theory would carry too much weight in the scientific world.

I became increasingly convinced, as I brooded, that *I* most certainly would have thought of a wheel; *I* would not have lounged around the centuries so long, content with an infantile dawn stone; starting from scratch, in fact, I would have . . . What would I have done . . . ? A familiar baffled feeling rose slowly to the surface from the depths of my subconscious: I was a castaway on my latest desert island, and I could make butter without a churn, knew all about breadfruit, blubber and sturgeons' bladders — but I didn't have a goat or a gun, or, *worst of all, a knife.* . . . How did one go about making a knife? Steel — where was it, and how in heaven's name did one forge it? *Papa Robinson had not told me; what would I do?*

Some other time I'll think about it, I caught my mind protesting according to the long-forgotten childhood formula; but this time I was not a child; it was too late (or rather, too early) to worry about steel — I should have looked it up in the encyclopedia thirty years ago — for this was the desert island of existence, and flintstone was my medium. I was Man, and had just risen, unsteadily, to my hind feet, leaving my forefeet free to deal with more immediate problems than swinging through the forest for I was finding the winds at the Dawn of Time decidedly cool; worse, it looked as though another of those glaciers was approaching; my own personal fur had been thinning out for several centuries too, and if evolution was going to go on this way I would have to have some more. I must, therefore, kill an animal, skin it, scrape it, then *wear* it. . . . What should I do all this *with?* I had no access to a handily wrecked ship, no Swiss mother's reticule to dive into and come up with a pair of scissors, a needle, or a bag of oats even — this time I was really on my own . . . without even a How To Do It book on flint-knapping. But as I was not a man I would have to do a little recasting: I was prehistoric Woman, and my man had run off with another, or gone on a prolonged hunting trip, leaving me to fend for myself and carve out my own existence. How would I do it in that empty early world? Pick up a stone, of course, and bring it down on the head of a slow-moving three-toed giant sloth. Sloths looked as though they had nice warm coats, and would provide dinner as well. Silly to use this blunt stone for scraping — bang it on a rock and make it sharper; now bang more judiciously; why not pick up another stone and bang it with that — after all you have *two* hands, haven't you? And we'll need a nice sharp knife for cutting a roast off the carcass. . . . Later, when winter comes, we'll spend the long evenings, snug in a cave before the fire, thinking all sorts of thoughts about improving the lot of prehistoric man as we pressure-flake some rather exquisite blades. . . .

Daydreaming as of old, so I instructed my Stone Age counterpart, carefree and excited at the project: I would start learning to flint-knap tomorrow. It would not take me long to master the technique. After all, if Neanderthal Man, whom some anthropologists will not even admit to the *Homo sapiens* fraternity, could show such ingenuity and artistry, surely so could I, a product of the twentieth century, with a supposedly normal intelligence.

I read about Stone Age implements and the scanty information available on the manufacture thereof with great attention and purpose that night; there was no procrastination to the encyclopedia this time — after all, my hypothetical survival was at stake.

Then, thinking about it next morning, under the hair dryer, where I think best, it seemed that it would be far more interesting and more of a challenge to equalize the number of working apprenticeship hours that I would have to spend in order to achieve Neanderthal Man's standards of flint-knapping with an anthropological time scale of achievement: this should prove once and for all that a ridiculously unnecessary number of centuries had been wasted. By a most complicated system, I started off with an ancestor who had left evidence of his occupation in Abbeville, France, some four hundred and fifty thousand years ago, then equalized these years with my own hopes of life expectancy translated into hours (it is most disconcerting at middle age to see your life reduced to hours — there are not nearly as many left as one had hoped). I am not very good at arithmetic, and there was consequently a lot of give and take to make things work out more evenly and easily, such as giving myself an extra ten years of the psalmist's three score and ten because of antibiotics, then the progress being made with plastic heart valves, artificial kidneys, etc., seemed to warrant a few more, until finally I allowed myself the life expectation of a centenarian, and with some relief, as it was a far more manageable figure to render into hours. All sorts of complications arose about the years already spent without any practical experience in flint-knapping, but these were eventually balanced against the slower development of my ancestor's brain pan, which I rather patronizingly decided was pint-sized to my quart (fortunately for my ego the size of Cro-Magnon Man's brain was then unknown to me: "approximately 1600 cc. for the male, compared with the present day average of 1500 cc.").

Abbeville Man, therefore, and Burnford Woman started out as equals on their survival course, castaways on the desert island of evolution, about to carve out our civilization from the materials to hand. I have given all the details of my Scale of Progressive Achievement in case someone else would like to benefit from them.

It was now the end of October and fortunately still quite warm for this part of the world. I found a sheltered dip in a sandbank at the end of one quarry and set to work; Raimie, now a very primitive form of Jackal, and looking as morose about his new role as ever, beside me. The first few thousand years were a pushover: an hour's banging of a hunk of jasper against a rocky outcrop on the quarry bed produced a fairly sophisticated dawn stone which would have dealt quite adequately with a three-toed sloth, and later, if I were not too particular about the scraping of his skin, provide me with a warm furry outfit, and something to gnaw on for a day or two as well. Well pleased with myself, I went in search of a hammer-stone for the next stage, nobly resisting the temptation to use the ready-made one that had tumbled out in my jackpot find. By the time I found a suitable stone most of the afternoon had gone, and so, of course, had several hundred years; worse still, I had completely wasted them, for my hammerstone turned out to be a clumsy failure (I am ashamed to admit that it split as well: my quart-sized brain pan had not selected the right material), and I had to fall back on my ancestor's stone. By dusk I was still banging frantically away, racing the centuries, until I realized at last, and Raimie whined his dismal agreement because he was hungry and wanted to go home for his supper, that this sense of urgency must be controlled: after all even Zinjanthropus Man, whose methods I was trying to master, had to eat and sleep — he was not just an automatic artifact-manufacturing machine. For all anybody knew about him, in fact, he was still furry enough to have hibernated a good part of his life away in his dank glacial cave. I must lead a normal life therefore, and confine my evolutionary activities to the afternoons. And a Good Thing Too, common sense was quick to add, if I did not want them confined to a padded cell. I must grow apace up the centuries, and equate time out of mind.

I do not really care to admit how long it took me to produce my first recognizable hand ax with the hammerstone. I doubt if it would have hewed down a raspberry cane; a Pleistocene four-year-old could probably have done better, and without macerating its fingers either. My scraper was better and would have produced quite a supple saber-toothed tiger tunic, I think; or, if Raimie had co-operated, a nice Primitive Jackal rug for the youngest Zinjanthropus child; but perhaps I cheated a little by using a piece of jasper that was naturally fractured into a fairly reasonable shape to start with, and only needed a little touching up here and there. At least I wasn't Eolithic Woman any more after these results: I was using *both* my hands, and soon my little red-rimmed anthropoid eyes would be peering around from under my shaggy, receding forehead, about to light, any century now, upon a splinter of bone or wood; then clumsily, wobblingly, with many contemporary grunts of pain and exasperation as it slipped on the smooth jasper surface, bang it with the hammerstone: two hands, and *three* things to control. I was really progressing.

There was no really hard wood available in the quarry, but there was a magnificent selection of bones from the moose, deer or bear carcasses dumped there over the years. For the first time Raimie showed some enthusiasm for my project when I helped myself to some, and he quickly followed my example. I was later most grateful for his interest, as his slow, thoughtful chewing rewarded me with some ready-made bone tools of a far more manageable size than I could produce myself.

Stage 2, coping with so many things at once, turned out to be unbelievably hard to master; I suspected Zinjanthropus of still having prehensile toes and using those as well. I was trying for an ovoid blade; we had dozens in the collection, ranging from "finely worked on all edges" to "coarsely worked on both surfaces with crudely scalloped edges." I was not setting my sights higher than the latter — and to be honest they barely got off the ground: eventually I graduated myself from the class of 50,000 B.C. only because the days were growing shorter and colder, and I thought that if I did not allow myself to shamble off soon and register in the Neanderthal School of Advanced Flint-Knapping I would still be in the Stone Age when I reached the age of ninety — according to the Burnford Scale of Progressive Ability. Forward, then to pressure flaking. . . .

Mary Tudor said that "Calais" would be found graven on her heart when she was dead. I know just how she felt, for "pressure flaking" will be found on mine. I tried and tried; and as the long-dead leaves whirled and skittered down the quarry and piled up inch by inch in nooks and crannies, I used them to start fires to warm my purple, trying hands, and tried again. Later I used the fires for experimental purposes too. I used to think a lot as I chipped my days away in my gravel pit, the centuries blowing past

me on the wind that carried a portent of snow now.
Far back behind the mists of time, Man had progressed beyond these intricacies of flint-knapping
which I could not master now, on a day when space
capsules were orbiting my world, and present-day
Man would soon be starting from scratch on the
bleakest desert island of the lot, the moon; my hairy-
fisted, dangling-armed, prognathous-jawed ancestor
had gone on to the bow and arrow and learned all by
himself how to smelt copper for his arrow tips, and
make fish hooks and gaffs from copper, too; all by
himself he had thought of pottery and agriculture,
religion, belief, morals and art — *all by himself*, with
no pontifications or guidance from the Swiss Family
Robinson or the How To Do It books; all this he
had done, and I could not even pressure-flake myself
out of my prehistoric cave. I knew that the Battle
of Bannockburn was fought in 1314, the square on
the hypotenuse equaled something or other, I could
ride a bicycle, decline some irregular verbs and make
a charlotte russe — but to what avail? I could not
pressure-flake. The world would have spun out the
centuries without my contributing one drop of cul-
tural oil to its axis. But, until the snow came, I would
not give up trying.

One of the books had hinted vaguely that possibly
extremes of heat and cold were used, so I baked pieces
of jasper like potatoes in my fire and when they were
red hot raked them out and let droplets of water fall

on them from a gull's feather. No result. I reversed
the procedure, cheating in a way, by freezing jasper
in the Deepfreeze at home, then applying a red-hot
knitting needle stuck through a cork handle (I rec-
onciled the Deepfreeze with the glacier, but realize
there was no moral justification for the knitting
needle). No result, except of course a burned finger,
but I was expecting that. I found a very clear picture
in a book of Ancient Man sitting on a log, placidly
applying pressure with a long stick to a stone clutched
between his useful toes. The pressure was being applied from his chest as he bent over, and his chest
was protected by a curved piece of wood, or possibly it was a human scapula, neatly lashed to the
top of the stick. Again I cheated miserably to gain
this effect: I used a vintage shooting-stick with a
double handle that opened out into a leather seat
which made a most comfortable chest protector, and
the ferrule was handily tipped with steel. But the results of this long-range flaking were equally dispirit-
ing, and, until I substituted boots for moccasins, painful as well. Closer work, which needed about the
same control and action as whittling wood, fared no
better.

It was becoming very cold indeed. Now strange
furtive people appeared occasionally in my hitherto
solitary quarry, and dumped their loads of garbage.
They came as harbingers of winter, confident that
the snow would cover up their misdeeds and the "No

Dumping" sign. They met with Raimie's full approval and he spent many happy hours checking over items. Sometimes I wandered over to join him and stretch my stiffening legs (I knew now why Java Man showed osteoarthritic changes in his thigh bones — the first recorded case of occupational disease), and I used to think about the humus gathering slowly through the centuries to obliterate the piles of tins and tires and bottles, until some archaeologist a thousand years from now dug down and rediscovered us. "Heinz Man" we would probably be termed, which saddened me, and the little Old Dutch Cleanser Woman would be exhibited in a museum as a fertility symbol perhaps, with controversies raging about the significance of her pointed cap, which saddened me even more. I hoped my little pile of chips and fragments of pre-Neanderthal culture, found at the same level beneath the humus of the future, would throw them into utter confusion. How humiliating it would be if they labeled them Eolithic — I redoubled my efforts.

My efforts would have made my Neanderthal teacher weep. I could have wept myself at my inadequacy. It was obvious that my very generous allowance of a hundred years' life expectancy would not even be enough for A.D. to appear on my tombstone at the rate I was progressing, and Raimie would still be roaming the tundra in a pack if the Burnford Scale was an accurate criterion.

Mercifully the snow came and put an end to my humiliation. We watched it cover the hills and ridges and quarries of the site, I sadly, Raimie joyfully, safely concealing until the spring thousands of as yet undiscovered artifacts, and releasing me from the pressure of the centuries.

I brooded now over the vast collection laid out in rows in the basement at home, arranging, rearranging, learning, discovering, wondering, pondering. And the more I pondered the progress of civilization the more humbled I became. I reviewed myself dispassionately, sitting there, surrounded by the handiwork of my ancestors: all that I knew about I had been taught, or knew by hearsay. I had never invented anything, never progressed; things that I had thought sometimes were uniquely inspired always turned out to have been invented long ago, sometimes thousands of centuries ago. I remembered my disillusionment as a child when I thought I was the first to discover that strong sunlight and a magnifying glass could make paper smolder, then burst into flames. Icarus was not more cast down than I to learn how belated was my discovery. I remembered the long hours — millenniums really — spent trying to invent a simple penny-in-the-slot machine from cardboard: it was supposed to vend one toffee, but it seldom did; either a plethora of toffees poured out along with the paper clips, pieces of Meccano and hairpins of its most intimate innards or else the drawer jammed and there were none (yet the model on the village railway station, so ancient that it looked as though it should have been in a museum along with the Bronze Age specimens, never divulged a thing without a penny in its maw, no matter how one shook and rattled the drawer). And I remembered how for years I thought I was unique in perceiving the miraculous fit of a dog or cat's coat, with its two precisely planned, unraveling slits in the exactly right locations for the eyes — until many years later I read that someone had commented on this marvel in a book. Even the homemade gunpowder fuse with which my brother and I blew up my dollhouse at some diabolic stage of childhood had been old hat to the Chinese when my more immediate ancestors had still been running around in woad. Sadly I faced the ultimate awful truth of my childhood's daydreaming and its present day counterpart: I would have perished within the week on my desert island or in the first era of evolution, without the Swiss Family Robinson or the How To Do It books.

It was small consolation to remind myself that I had never been Ancient Man but Ancient Woman; for Woman, as far as I knew, had never invented anything beyond recipes, cosmetics and clothing, from the evolutionary word "Go" until Madame Curie — I had hoped for better things from me. It suddenly struck me with a terrible shock that Woman, in fact, would still be back in the dawn stone days if it had not been for Man: the textbooks barely mentioned her except as a chattel who stoked the fire, cared for Man and produced his children. Sometimes she was portrayed gnawing an obviously inferior bone or stringing seashells in her leisure time, and one book shyly suggested that she may have been responsible for pottery. One might have thought that if her main purpose in life, since life began, was procreation, she could at least have contributed a few of the major advancements in handling this subject several centuries before Man, goaded into action by realizing what a bungle she was making of this simple job of providing his heirs, steeping herself in superstition, passivity and ignorance, stepped in and invented chloroform, forceps, antisepsis and Grantly Dick Read. Poor Woman — what a dull, unchanging picture she presented down the ages: stoking, producing, caring for; how she had blossomed and invented in the last fifty years was little short of an evolutionary miracle. I looked at myself with a new respect (even although I secretly knew after recent evidence that I should not really be here for another several thousand years).

A simple, mentally chastened woman now, fresh from my Pleistocene cave, I looked around the house with new wonder: what brilliant mind conceived, planned and executed *hinges* for example? I Hoovered the house in reverence and awe over all the things that went on inside that machine. I stirred a sauce (consider inventing a sauce) and my mind reeled at

the intellectual processes that had produced the spat-
ula — the latex from the trees, the mold, the mold
machinery (every last little cog of it), the plastic
handle. . . . And at the limitless horizons, like childhood's void of sky, that stretched before me at the
thought of *plastic* and the mind that gave it birth, I
felt quite faint. . . . Some other time, I thought tiredly,
some other time I'll think about plastic.

Someone should explore the psychological benefits
of my experiment: flint-knapping your way up the
years of your life from the moment of birth to the
present day must be a far better and more economical
therapy than lying on a couch merely recalling them.
Think of all the repressions that must be released
with the banging, and the good healthy outdoor exercise into the bargain; the moment of truth at the end;
the mental stock-taking. I speak from experience: not
only did I emerge from my Pleistocene cave clutching my graduation scraper, but I took my place in
present-day civilization again considerably humbled,
facing the fact squarely that the wheel would have
continued to go uninvented on the North American
continent by me, and finding endless cause for re-
newed wonder and delight — a pencil sharpener or a
tin of sardines for example — in the world around me.

But not only that, I blew the highly harmful Swiss
Family Robinson, who had started the whole business in the first place, right out of my subconscious
and onto the top of the first island that appeared as

the water level dropped over the world and Noah was looking for a landfall. I blew them, sans goat, guns or knife; sans reticule (and I meanly totaled up the number of things they would miss without this: according to my calculations Mrs. Swiss Robinson would have had to pay excess baggage on a first-class air fare); sans even the clothes they swam ashore in and all the ridiculously unnecessary paraphernalia with which they had cluttered up every island I had shared with them, and I left them to work their own way up through the dawn stones, and see how they liked it. . . . The therapy was complete.

The winter has passed, and even now the snow is receding from that ancient workshop site; pick points, burins, scrapers, blades and hand axes will soon be peeping through again in company with scyllas and crocuses. Somewhere down East the dust is swirling round museum basements and the archaeologists are setting the wheels in motion that will bring them to the Lakehead to make planned scientific digs in un-disturbed areas; carbon 14 tests will be applied to charcoal, fossils and bones; artifacts will gather and multiply and be grouped and regrouped; learned re-ports will be written with a wealth of scientific cau-tion, peppered with possibles, probables and perhapses. They may inspect our thousand-odd specimens, and I hope to be there if they do, for I have infiltrated my best scraper and hand ax; and if they pass muster un-

detected I shall look upon this as an official matricula-
tion from Stage 2, the Zinjanthropus School.

And as the returning warmth of the sun increases
I hasten to write this, my own personal unscientific
report: partly to remember the unique enchantment
of the centuries I passed last fall on my quiet hillside,
with my patient Primitive Jackal; and partly, remembering the disillusionment of the magnifying glass, the
dog's coat, the toffee vendor and the gunpowder, and
a thousand other things that were never to be mine
alone, I want to be quite sure that no one else beats
me to the post with a psycho-archaeological-anthropo-
logical report on a Pleistocene beach site, such as
this . . .

Inclinations to Fish

EVEN on those first holidays by the seashore that traditionally braced the very young of my day, fishing lines and shrimping nets were as natural a part of our background as spades, buckets, inflatable animals and sand in the sandwiches; and from then on it seems that the first consideration given in all subsequent family holidays was to the fishing amenities. So, as the twig is bent, did I incline naturally towards water; and grew up regarding all large bodies of it as potential fish containers, to be used as a means to that end. I learned to swim in it at as tender an age as possible in order not to inconvenience anyone if I fell off the end of the jetty or out of a boat while fishing; and I learned to handle a boat in order to fish from further out. It was always there, the waters of seas, rivers and lochs, as adults never failed to point out to children foolish enough to say there was nothing to do; even when it was raining it was still there, possibly even improved, just waiting for idle hands to test their skill in the depths.

My daughters, on the other hand, despite the fact that they have been brought up within free and easy range of some of the finest fishing on this continent, regard similar large bodies of water only as convenient surfaces, fluid in summer, solid in winter, on which to sail, ski or drive. I had given up all hope that my own satisfyingly filled pool of memories could be similarly stocked in my daughters': there are plenty of Isaak Walton's "Brothers of the Angle" in this part of the world, but very few Sisters — and as for teenage ones they appeared to be extinct. Until this year when I found a note, the text of which must be the most universally commonplace of all time, but which so astonished and delighted me that I have added it to my collection of rare "Have gone . . ." notes left for me over the years (". . . to eat Joan's Grandmother; . . . to see man about Horse Julie," etc.). This one said, quite simply, "Have gone Fishing." It was the first of many.

And so I write for that one who went fishing, in the warm hope that one day she may add her own chapter to it; one distant day when she perhaps has daughters of her own, and they in turn regard large bodies of water from yet another dimension, driving their nuclear-powered sports submarines through it perhaps, or diving down in aqualungs to Cousteau-inspired marine resorts; but, although times and places and dimensions will change, the fish will always be there, and where there are fish there will be fishers, and children even then will surface to leave the same "Have gone . . ." note. And whether they go with spear or fly rod, hook and line, or even hands, it will not matter: the reward will be the same.

The catch itself is almost unimportant. The real reward lies eventually in the associate memories — certainly anything exciting, dramatic or outstanding in mine seem to have an invariable connection with fish, either singly or in quantities. My father being struck by lightning, for example, while wielding his rod in Shetland (and the awe with which one subsequently regarded his providential rubber waders); the rusty hook buried in my brother's hand while flounder-fishing off the east coast (a pause here to explain this drama in terms of pre-penicillin days): the vicious teeth of the huge conger eels we hooked in the flooded coastal slate quarries, snapping in a sporadic reflex action long after they had been well and truly clouted on their ugly heads, and which we had been warned could remove a finger as neatly as a chopper. A more tranquil operation was shrimping at low tide, one that called for no courage or talent, and often held unexpected bonuses of sand eels, rusted telescopes, or crabs in the nets; and the story that someone had once found a sixpence in the "purse" of a crab always filled one with the undiminished prospecting hope of striking a similar vein. Low tide, too, on Pleinmont in Guernsey, was a time for feeling around behind the seaweed curtain fronds

of rock crevices, until living tentacles, eerily purpose-
ful in their invisible groping, met and clasped the
blind apprehensive fingers in response, then twined
strongly about the wrist — to their undoing, for then
the little octopus could be tugged out, blowing indignant jets of ink as it came. The less squeamish
among us mastered the art of turning them inside out
for the pot.

The only nightmare fishing memories stem from
the days when we trolled off the island of Luing in
Argyllshire, within sound of Coirebreachan, the great
whirlpool. If it was an ebb tide and the wind in the
right quarter, its hungry hollow roar with the sinister accompaniment of howling crosscurrents seemed
to fill the world and me with unreasoning terror.
My imagination, well primed on "A Descent into the
Maelström" and "The Merry Men," worked over-
time: sails tore free, oars were lost, and helpless boats
drifted down, swirling in ever faster and smaller
circles until at last they were sucked down forever
into that terrible vortex. . . . I had, of course, carefully studied the recommended courses of action for
such a predicament: one invoked the Trinity, or
threw over a three-legged stool, or three hairs plucked
from a virgin (or was it three virgins? I could never
track down the source of my information here). A
practical child, it always seemed to me that, win or
lose, whatever one threw out there was bound to be
a material loss, whereas invocations could only lead

to spiritual gain; so I secretly turned myself into a kind of prophylactic human prayer wheel all the time I fished, and every gust of wind that carried that terrifying primeval cry in my direction spun involuntary invocations from me. I was convinced then — and still am — that it was only by my ceaseless revolutions that we ever returned safely to shore.

Of course not all memories were born of drama and excitement; mostly they were of the sunlit, indefinable essence of a happy childhood, distilled from a satisfying compound of many similar experiences; so that if I look back and see a small boat sailing through a shoal of mackerel and two children hauling in the silvery fish one after another on lines baited with yellow wool I know that it is a timeless composite. So, too, were the piers when the herring fleet came in, the cobbles shiny and slippery with scales soon after; the shouted incomprehensible repartee of the rubber-booted fisher lasses, with their skirts kilted up under sacking aprons, their high fresh coloring, brawny freckled arms, and flashing swift knives, the gulls fighting and screaming overhead for their reward; and, like a lively steady accompaniment to the crescendo of birds and voices, I hear the slap-slap-slapping of the herring landing in a silver arc from the knives to the waiting boxes, and the air is filled for me again with the clean salt tang of bonnie, halesome farin' fish, tarry ropes, seaweed and salt-damp wool. . . . So vivid is this picture still over the years that there have been times when the gulls have risen, screaming, in the middle of the night, from a little lake in the very heart of this continent; and in that moment between sleeping and waking I have thought to open my eyes on a sunlit cobbled pier again, and have known no greater desolation than finding only an alien blackness, and the tame lapping of fresh water, forever captive in its shores.

I came to know many fishermen, for I haunted the piers wherever I was in the hopes of being taken out in a trawler or smack, or even a motorboat, or for assistance with ever fouled and snarled equipment. I never met with anything but the same tolerant patience, from the ruddy round-faced stalwarts of the east coast, with their hospitable mugs of black stewed tea and ambrosial meals of fish-and-chips (still piping hot in their vinegary newspaper) or succulent kippers, to the tall, reserved patois-speaking islanders of the south, with their silky-smooth close-knitted guernseys and the little gold ring in one ear; or, later, the stocky, smocked Bretons, garrulous and cheerful, with their incapacitating Calvados-and-crab hospitality. I thought it was the most romantic occupation in the world: sailing away to the west as the sun went down, and being able to spit clear across the decks, harvesting your livelihood from the depths of the sea in nets that surely must hold the same breathless excitement of the unknown as my shrimping one; and rolling, godlike in your thigh boots, into the King's Arms on

your return. I longed to share it, and the knowledge
that at most I could only hope to grow up into one
of the wives or sweethearts who waited for their return, or "moaned at the bar" (which for years I
thought was in the King's Arms as well) was one
of childhood's deep despairs.

It was a rare day indeed if they ever took me any
farther to sea than the end of the harbor, but more
often than not they made up for my disappointment
with a variety of treats that ranged from filling my
pail with bait or fish to pulling the cord for the steam
whistle on a trawler; from inspecting the ship's cat's
kittens and the mate's photographs of his sweetheart
to learning how to darn or to crack a crab. While I
grieve sometimes that my children have grown up
without a similar heritage of the sea, I grieve even
more that they will never have known the fishermen
of that world, with their infinite patience, courtesy
and unfailing kindness to children, for theirs was a
likeness every child should be privileged to know.
Above all I would have had them know the enchantment of a childhood that included Donald-the-Fish-
erman. . . .

For they came and went, the men of fleets and
town harbors, with a bustling, businesslike regularity;
but Donald was different and was always there, a
solitary toiler of the sea against the lonely wild grandeur of the Western Isles, to whom time meant nothing except in terms of tides, and, on and off, Eternity.

The long days with him were the ones that I loved most of all, that were not concerned with rods or lines or nets, but wicker creels — the days when I went out with him to his lobster grounds and helped him haul the creels in, then set them again with chunks of eel or dogfish, while all around the round-eyed football heads of curious seals bobbed up and watched us at work: they were sailors and fishermen who had drowned long ago, said Donald, who, like most of his calling, could not swim a stroke himself. He was all I ever wanted to be — a fisherman, and a teller of stories besides; a come-day-go-day-God-send-Sunday West Highlander, gentle and dreaming. How to describe the mounting anticipation of those years when we drove up the road that wound among the sea lochs, grinding our way up Rest-and-Be-Thankful in something with side curtains called a Bianchi; nearer and nearer, past the old graveyard with the queer little prehistoric stone figure that pivoted on a flat tombstone, that was supposed to point the location of the next grave, and was sometimes there, and sometimes mysteriously not; over the little hump-backed bridge which somebody never failed to inform the others was the only one that spanned the Atlantic, and on beyond to the little whitewashed village that crouched between the hills and the sea — and Donald. And all the time the burning question was: had he been Saved or not in the intervening year? "Saved," that is, by one of the Evangelistic missions who periodically made the rounds of the Highlands, with a portable harmonium, setting up business on the village green, there to pluck penitent brands from the burning — having first fanned the flames under them with hair-raising tracts that threatened eternal combustion to unheeding sinners. We could always tell at once: when Donald had been plucked, he came slowly over the rocks to greet us, his face long and gloomy; life, we would find out later, was real and earnest, strong drink a mocker, and the Pit yawning for those who profaned the Sabbath with worldly pleasure (such as playing a Gramophone, or sailing to the Island of Sheep for picnics, or fishing with us). When we went out for the lobsters together I would listen enraptured as he expounded further on the stern doctrine that now ruled his gentle soul, and related the horrid fates that awaited those who did not mend their ways; drowned sailors and fishermen no longer returned to the sea as happy seals — ninety-nine per cent of them, one gathered, were sizzling away in the Pit instead, in company with sinful landlubbers. Not that any such fate would ever overtake me, he always hastened to assure me, for I was a child; and by some deep Donaldian logic, children were exempt forever, even when they grew up, simply because they were children now. (Many years later I was to read about Tir nan Og, the Land of Youth that lies eternally below the legendary Celtic horizon — so far below, it seems, that it missed the searching beam of rampant mission theologians.)

Other years he would bound happily over the rocks, his brown fine-boned face ironed out once more to its familiar gentle expression, his dark blue eyes twinkling with pleasure, and he would be mercifully (for us) lost to the fold once more; and, forbye, chust be having a wee glass of spirits perhaps with Himself. . . . Then, instead of that gloomy vengeful world of Jehovian wrath, I would hear again of enemy submarines surfacing in lonely sea lochs, of Q ships, wrecks and prize money, strange fish and wandering mines caught in nets, and stranger characters, his soft Highland voice with the beautiful turn of phrase of the storyteller who translates from the Gaelic as he goes.

"No life so pleasant as that of the *well governed* angler," said Isaak Walton, that shrewd fount of fishy philosophy, who was and is my delight, and although he doubtless drew a line between angling for pleasure and fishing for a living, the moral is compleat for both. How Donald would have baffled him — his life so content (save only for those times when the professional fishers of souls were casting in his direction), his fish so fair and plentiful, and he the least well governed of all the fishermen I ever knew. He was a master of the makeshift, and when, with the passing of the years, stopgap repairs in the boat reached permanent status, all were joyfully declared to be even

better than the original; the piece of driftwood that
so exactly wedged the tiller and doubled as a row-
lock pin, the tear in the sail that was so "handy to
keek through." He always seemed to "happen" upon
whatever he was in need of at the crucial moment,
and none was ever more surprised or delighted than
he to come upon it: each piece of equipment providentially rolling into view from the uttermost depths
of the bow locker, each ideal hook or weight of the
moment happened upon under the floorboards, was
greeted like a long-lost friend. The boat leaked, and
he dealt with this by stopping the hole in the bailer
with an ingenious tinker's plug cut from a tobacco
tin; and when I lost this masterpiece overboard he
dug around in the locker and came up with a syrup
tin that was so much better that it was still in use
last time I saw him. The Highland half of me was
completely in its impractical transcendent element,
but every now and then the other half of stern Norman with a dash of canny Lowlander feebly tried
to assert itself with orderly compartmented boxes,
hooks safely embedded in corks, and neatly coiled
lines: the result of this, like every other battle of
heredities, far from being one of Well Government,
was systematic chaos, out of which I never emerged
then or since.

This chaos was as much a part of me as a shell to
a snail, and, as long as I stayed in my natural bar-
baric background of coarse salt-water fishing I never

even noticed it. In fact I would probably have felt
quite lost if I had not had to deal with the normal
conspiracy of lines that writhed into tight enduring
knots at my approach, hooks that homed to my
clothes like vampires to a feast, or rusty reels that
fed on fingertips. Anyway, any old line, tangled or
not, any old hook baited with limpet or cheese or
anything handy, was acceptable to saithe; mackerel
were not very particular either, or herring; no skill
was needed with eels, only darkness, depth and courage; and any fool could shrimp. It was when I had
bouts of ambition and tried to thrash my savage way
into the rarefied civilization of the angling world, the
skillful well-governed world of fly fishing inhabited
by my relations and friends, that my chaos became
an obstruction, and morally as well as physically.
Separated from makeshift, *mañana* and make-do; mad-
dened by fiddly little flies that unknotted and lost
themselves from even fiddlier casts every time my back
was turned — if they were not lodged malevolently in
some inaccessible twig or crevice; dismally flailing the
waters with the subtlety of a beaver smacking the
surface with its tail, with an evil rod that obviously
hated me — sooner or later the thin veneer of civilization would crack, and I would be covertly digging for beyond-the-pale worms. The plump ones
could be drawn like a sock over a hackled fly, I found,
the line then weighted with a stone, or even a brass
reefer button in extreme (this is very successful,

probably because of its attractive shininess), then the shameful lure dropped furtively into a safely remote pool. I was quite proud of the unique casting skill I developed for low water, landing my worm at the top of little rivulets between stones and rocks, so that it rolled with realistic allure, and only sorry that it had to go unrecognized. (It is no good sending a worm whistling through the air, by the way, for they fly off very easily, even those as well upholstered as mine: a gentle sideways sling is much more effective. And never use winged flies under a worm: they never look quite the same again.) Crime seemed to come easily to me, for I never forgot to remove all evidence from the fly or investigate the interior of my catch for incriminating segments.

I became, by necessity, a solitary angler, successful only when out of sight, and as such have many pleasant, immoral memories, whereas all those concerned with brown or speckled trout with an honest fly in their mouths seem uniformly gloomy. I recall without enthusiasm subdued and fruitless hours spent in the too-close company of the dry fly, wet fly, split cane heaven-born; days on the hallowed waters of a fishing lodge in Galloway, implacably imprisoned in a boat; haunted, nerve-wracked days with gregarious anglers, unshakable enthusiasts, forever converging unexpectedly over a hillside or around a bend in the river, dogged in their determination to "see how you are getting on." I would prefer not to dwell on the grim and ghastly trout that got away from my flies; only on that golden procession of memorable fish who got away from worms, caterpillars, beetles or even bacon; and that even more radiantly happy (and flagrantly unlawful) procession that got away from my hands and snares and sharpened sticks, or made their escape from the shallows into which I had chased them, some form of knobkerrie in hand. That they did not get away from dynamite, or from that ingenious forerunner of automatic devices, a domestic duck or goose harnessed to my line and towing my bait through the water, was probably only because neither was available.

Strangely enough, it was a friend of my father's who initiated us one Sunday afternoon in the Border country into the most primitive of all the water poacher's arts: taking trout by hand alone, or "guddling." I say "strangely enough," because by some deep interpretation of the unwritten rules that curled the lip at the lowly worm on one hand, the Angling Establishment seemed to consider this method quite socially acceptable on the other, and I could have pursued it quite openly in their view. Unfortunately, water bailiffs and keepers interpreted the sport less feudally — for the desire or necessity to guddle only seemed to arise by private and preserved waters — thereby forcing it underground, along with my worms. One lay on the bank of the burn, still and quiet, shadows cast behind, while the hand gently, apparently aimlessly, drifted downstream towards the quarry pulsating dreamily in the shadows under the bank or the roots of a tree; then gently, so gently, the moment of contact, and the forefinger moving to and fro across the belly of the fish. This soothing stroking, or "tickling," was supposed to send the fish into a witless trance, when the patient hand eased infinitesimally upward, still tickling, until the moment when finger and thumb snapped together over the gills. I never had any real success with guddling then, or after, although I spent many hours at it: either the fish were never in a place where my arm was long enough to reach them, or else I was too clumsy in my impatient approach: I would get them half out of the water sometimes, only to lose them, and of course this only whetted my appetite further.

Years later in England, however, riding home across a stretch of Exmoor one summer evening, Belinda, the pony, ambled along the banks of a stream, so that I had a clear view down into the water; and suddenly I could see Jimmy Tweedie stretched out by the burn in Scotland against an almost identical background of moorland, stunted trees and chuckling peaty brown water; and I had an overwhelming urge to try my luck at guddling again. I had some trouble with Belinda: when I lay down on the bank above a likely looking place she plodded after on bank-shaking hooves and huffed and puffed and drooled down the back of my neck. There was nothing to

tether her to — only bog myrtle and whin bushes, so
finally I waded over to the other bank. I walked
downstream on one side and she followed inquisi-
tively on the other. When I stopped she stopped,
and when I gazed into the water she gazed too,
her elegant little ears twitching with interest, reflected distractingly immediately below me. It was
unnerving: no one should attempt to guddle with
a horse. But at last I came to a place wide enough
to be rid of those ears, and I saw several dark forms
streak away at my approach, so I stretched out on
the bank to wait. It all happened just as it should, a
streamlined shadow gradually visible, drowsing in the
deeper shadow of the overhang, and my hand drifted
downstream almost as though it had no part of me
until my fingers, light as a butterfly (I found it much
easier to be a butterfly in these waters, freed of the
thought of a lurking keeper), brushed against the fish,
to and fro, until it rose, almost purring with pleasure,
up towards the surface. I do not know how I got it
out, but still dream of the moment — in a kind of
combined pounce, scoop and underhand pass. The
trout volleyed out of the water and landed several
feet back on the opposite bank, scoring a perfect goal
between Belinda's forelegs. She shied violently, one
hoof landed with as deadly an aim as my own on the
head of the fish, effectively stilling it, but jangling
her nerves even more. It was a most remarkable performance, and a handsome, sizable fish, although for

a while I wondered how I was going to hang on to it during a three-mile ride back to the farm, as I had no handkerchief or shoelaces or any other available material to thread through the gills. I had almost resigned myself to stuffing it down the front of my shirt when Belinda, as providentially as any piece of line happened upon by Donald, whisked her long tail before me: she obliged fairly graciously, and I plaited the three hairs into a handle. I rode back in triumph, and nothing ever tasted quite so delicious as that guddled trout, the culmination of many years' dishonest toil.

I was puzzled for a moment when I thought about that meal, for I seemed to recall every last bite of it in the hungriest detail, and could almost see the clean-picked bones on a willow pattern plate. Then I realized that I had probably not had any fresh fish for some time, living where I was on a remote moorland farm; and I know now from traumatic hungry experience that periodically I am overcome by an overwhelming craving for fish that reduces me, desperate as any dope addict, to a state of almost gibbering greed until it is satisfied. This gastronomic urge, this Fish Addiction, no less, obviously stems from early environment and diet, for I could dissect the backbone neatly out of a herring at an age when my own children were spooning up Junior Sieved Fish, and by the time they were embarked on Junior Chopped I was already paving the way to my addiction with the crustaceans: lobster and crab were commonplace as were crayfish, prawns and scallops; winkles, mussels and oysters were old friends. We have been brainwashed into accepting psychological explanations for almost any deviation from the normal nowadays, and childhood as the natural spawning ground from which they may be later fished: my ravening eccentricity would seem to tie up (most aptly too) into a nice watertight case in point. But I wonder if there could not be also some more basic, chemical, deep-seated dietary reason? Exiled koala bears, after all, pine away without their eucalyptus leaves, and no synthetic, scientifically balanced substitute will stay them; and so, I believe, do great big sturdy pandas without bamboo shoots — nothing else is really satisfactory. It would be as unbearable to me if I tried to get by on sardines and anchovies when my craving is at its worst. This always seems to happen in winter, and it is significant to my theory that fresh fish are then almost nonexistent locally, being frozen in and obtainable only through a hole in the ice after considerable outlay and privation, and most supplies that replace them come unappealingly frozen, thereby unconsciously reducing my intake to an apparent danger level. Or, when I have been separated too long from the sea, that longtime dietary source, so that when I return to my native shores for a visit, understanding friends and relations beat a path to the fishmonger's: breakfast, lunch and dinner — I am insatiable as a sea lion

for the first three or four days. If I am to include
an outstanding dietary memory here it is of the expression on the face of my hostess at a cocktail party
that once took place during those first crucial days
of homecoming, when she returned, fifty seconds too
late for the bowl of fresh shrimp which she had
foolishly left within my reach one minute before. If
she should ever read this I hope she will accept now
my belated apologies and explanation: it was not that
wretched couple some ten feet away on whom I gazed
with silent accusation and enigmatic lifted eyebrow
(and to whom I now apologize too): it was I alone,
in the grip of my desire, and silent because my mouth
was full. And while I am about it I might apologize
too to that most kindly unsuspecting host who took
me to Prunier's last year and was called to the tele-
phone halfway through his plate of oysters: you were
right to look so momentarily baffled on your return;
you *did* leave more than three; as a matter of fact you
left five.

I wish I knew too whether other coastal exiles, or
other twigs bent as I was towards water, then nur-
tured from sapling to tree on its bounty, show similar compulsive inclinations. It would be nice to know
that we were not simply greedy, but legitimately
hungry victims of circumstance. Perhaps that king
who so tragically overindulged himself on lampreys
was one; we might even find that our sympathies
were misdirected to those impetuous young Oysters

who trotted so trustingly after the Walrus and the Carpenter.

Probably not in my time, but eventually, as I now learn, the answer will be known. Just now I picked up a newspaper, which quotes a professor of biology to this fell effect: a day is coming when man will be inclined towards a fish diet by force of necessity for his survival; for, with 50,000,000 more human beings arriving in the world every year than departing from it, in the harvest of the waters alone lies the hope of "forestalling that time when the ominously expanding human population, even in the most favored lands, will run short of animal protein."

The thought of that day is saddening to me. Not morbidly sad because I will be absent — for the prospect of eating oysters to the sound of trumpets on Tir nan Og is infinitely more pleasing. Nor am I sentimentally sad that a pursuit which I have followed with so much happiness will no longer be "the pleasant curiosity of fish and fishing" but a stark reality. (Frankly I take a certain baleful pleasure in the thought that those mortifyingly purist anglers will have to come down to my own base practices . . . or risk a premature bestowal of that final accolade, "An Excellent Angler — now with God.") I do not feel an ancestral sadness for the plight of my descendants; there is nothing whatever I can do about it. But it is unbearably sad to sit here and watch the clock ticking away on its mad ratio of time, proteins, and potential fish-eaters. Infinitely more poignant than not being there is the fact that I will be circumstantially and gastronomically extinct.

These pages came into being because of a note left by my daughter, partly for my own nostalgic enjoyment, and partly to convey some of the delights in store for her. Because reminiscences do not like to be confined, but lead one from the other, I called these "Inclinations," claiming freedom to wander off down any side tracks of nostalgia, make any confessions or apologies, or come to any conclusions I fancied. Having rambled so far, I am dismayed to find my conclusion forced upon me. The biology professor has turned my idle reminiscence into a case history of one member of a vanishing species. And I feel trapped: tick-tock, every moment more decadent . . .

Considering the bleak prospect, however, that hangs over me and the whooping crane, I find it a keen incentive to evaluate an individual wealth of days, present assets, or the mounting interest on each passing moment. I count myself therefore fortunate beyond measure that so much of that wealth has been spent where and when it was, and that I never knew a time when it would have to be hoarded against the future; and that given such rare hindsight I can afford to be a reckless spendthrift in the soaring economy of the days to come.

And so I have only this left to say to my daughter: gather your own precious riches of waters while you may; squander your days among them; continue to scatter your Have Gone Fishing notes across the years. And cultivate the company of those whose "hearts are fitted for contemplation and quietness, men of mild, sweet and peaceable spirit — as indeed most anglers are," for the time will come when there are *not* as many good fish in the sea as ever came out of it.

Tom

═══

As the swallows to spring so was Tom to our northland winter: the sudden appearance in the garden of that sinister, underworld figure with the bristling, bull-necked head and cauliflower ears heralded the first heavy snowfall of the season within twenty-four hours. Where he came from remained a mystery; he brought with him an indefinable air of foreign parts, and he was certainly never seen around the neighborhood at any other season, yet he materialized with such casual accuracy of timing that one felt that he might have been waiting just around the corner for the moment. Heavy and deliberate, his massive low-slung shoulders swaying, he would swagger up the short drive to the garage; and some ten feet behind, furtive and thin in her shabby fur coat, came the timorous figure of his wife — at least, we awarded her this status after two years' constancy, but their true relationship remained as much of a mystery as their origins, and appeared to be entirely platonic.

Tom always took an unswerving course for the

warped board at the rear of the garage, but for the first day or so after his arrival he was wary about entering — he was casing the joint, the children said knowledgeably — and would crouch for minutes, with head and shoulders only in the opening, his companion keeping a nervous watch over his monumental rear. Then, inch by inch, the ugly striped body would disappear. If he had had a prosperous summer it was a tight squeeze. When the last inch of thick ringed tail had joined its owner, Mrs. Tom would allow a decent, respectful interval, then follow, slipping easily between the boards like a piebald wraith. Inside the garage the upturned sailing dinghy rested for the winter on trestles, and in the half-decked bow, dark and draughtproof, safe from ambush, they took up residence for the winter. There were other seemingly inviting and secure hideouts in the garage, behind the window screens, the cavernous depths under the tool-bench, on a pile of sacks behind a stacked barricade of flowerpots, or even up in the half-loft, but these were never even considered apparently. The sailing dinghy was their unchanging stronghold.

"Tom's back — snow's coming!" the children would say, rushing to check their skis and toboggans, for he was infallible. Every year they wooed him optimistically for the first few days, bearing succulent bones and morsels of fish to the garage; but however silently and suddenly they threw open the doors they were never able to catch a glimpse of the tenants, only that living taut silence that remains suspended after the abrupt complete cessation of movement, and very occasionally a hurried scrabbling of claws on wood. Sometimes they stood by the upturned hull, tapping and calling him forth to partake, but never did they receive any other acknowledgment than a savage spine-chilling growl; and if they were misguided enough to bend down and peer up into the hollow muffled blackness they were invariably greeted with a vicious hiss and a rapier thrust of razor claws. The children said generously that he timed these swipes to miss by a fraction, but I was not prepared to let them prove it after watching one hair-raising performance, and forbade any further attempts at direct communication. Four years' acquaintanceship flowered no confidence in Tom's benevolence either.

As long as the snow lasted they were our tenants, and tenants in the best tradition — clean and quiet and keeping themselves to themselves. They subsisted, I suppose, on the neighborhood garbage cans, on the few-and-far-between birds that remained — mostly house sparrows — and on our handouts. Although, even as I write that word I know that it is wrong: humble offerings, or even tributes, would be more correct. These offerings were accepted by Tom only if left on the ground and no one was in sight. If placed in a saucer they were left untouched. Yet on the extremely rare occasions when it was possible to catch more than a fleeting glimpse of her, it was noticed that Mrs. Tom was not above having a snack from a saucer, or even from the dog's dish. Even this slight concession to domesticity seemed out of character, for she was the most truly wild of the two. She had none of Tom's contemptuous disregard or savage scorn for humans, nor would she ever stand her ground upon an encounter with them; rather, she had all the self-effacing quality of the elusive wild creature: furtive, slipping away, fading silently into cover, and she had an almost chameleon ability to merge into the background. We knew she went abroad at night, the evidence in small solitary paw marks on the snow, and there were many lurid speculations in the family as to her destination; but other than those delicate imprints, for weeks at a time she was as disembodied as Tom was not. She left us in the same ephemeral way one year: no one could remember when they had last seen her, so no one ever knew when she was gone.

But Tom the Terrible sallied forth each morning to keep his domain safe from possible rival mobsters, and his presence was wind vane, weather prophet and timekeeper all in one: on the fence by breakfast time, unless the thermometer hovered at 12 degrees or below, his squat chunky back turned to the wind. He sat always on the same fence post by the lane, still and sinister as a medieval gargoyle crouched on a battlement; and any dog passing on a carefree garbage round down the lane would turn and double back on his tracks rather than venture below the cold yellow eyes of that feline gangster. We had two dogs at the time, a bull terrier who was a dedicated cat hunter — yet who lavished, strangely enough, all the affection of his belligerent heart upon his own beloved Siamese — and a large Labrador. Both dogs, from the day Tom moved in, treated the garage as though it were surrounded by an invisible fence at thirty feet, but they retained possession of the rest of the garden, and claimed the lane as a right of way where it passed to within a few feet of the garage. Tom, in return, stayed within his invisible boundary, and conceded their right of way along the lane by averting his head as the dogs passed below: eyes fixed ahead, tails high, they saw not, neither were they seen. No one will ever know what effort this must have cost the terrier, for he would start to quiver with suppressed rage fifty feet away; and no one will ever know why he allowed a stranger any living rights at all in his dominion, for his normal foreign policy was one of active aggression and persecution. But as far as I know the territorial pact was never broken.

Far more strangely, it was also adhered to by the Siamese, who by long association was the nearest possible thing to a feline bull terrier, and was the fearless match of any cat or dog. Only once did I see them meet, and that was by mistake. Each unaware of the other, they stalked the same bird from two different angles of the garage. Breathless, I watched from a window: it would be flyweight Siamese Simon against heavyweight Battling Tom when they met, but I thought that the odds might be equalized by the agility and cunning of the Siamese. Inch by suspense-filled inch they converged, their stalking tactics identical, until suddenly they came whisker to whisker at the corner: for one electrified minute blue and yellow eyes met in horrified astonishment. Then two sets of ears dropped simultaneously and both cats backed up and crouched with lowered heads and lashing tails. The Siamese took the initiative by stretching out each elegant dark-stockinged foreleg in turn, the pads flattened and opened to show his wicked curved claws. Not to be outdone, Tom displayed his weapons too. Here it comes, I thought, nose pressed to window, fascinated by the traditional jungle choreography of the performance. And then, as though puppets jerked by the same wire, both cats turned their heads sharply to their right, paused, as though waiting for the lights to turn, then trotted smartly off in different directions. Clearly it had been a territorial *faux pas* of first magnitude, but how I envied them the consummate feline aplomb that allowed them to deal with it so gracefully and diplomatically.

For four infallible leveling years Tom took up winter quarters with us, and his subsequent weather forecasts were as accurate as the timing of his arrival. "Temperature's dropping," one might say, noticing him leaving his post early; or "A false thaw soon,"

we would tell one another sagely, watching our
weather bureau stretching luxuriously and settling
down for a nap in the pale wintry sunshine. Then,
"It's spring — it must be!" the children said one year,
despite a Christmas card landscape, for they had seen
Tom, rarest of all sights, actually washing himself —
and not just the usual desultory lick, but a thorough
businesslike spring cleaning; and we uncovered the
snow from a sheltered bed and found the green spikes
of scyllas truly pushing through.

They were leveling years to me because there had
never before been an animal in my life, with whom
awareness was mutual, with whom I could not come
to some terms of trust or friendly recognition. But
Tom was my failure, even though I remained constantly blind to the level of defeat to which I was
reduced. I never stopped trying to win him to my
charitable bondage, hoping that if I captured his interest through his stomach, his heart would capitulate
in time as well; so blind that even when his stead-
fast snarling resistance should have shamed me long
before into recognizing his true dignity, I went on
trying. His unyielding scorn of the whole human
race triumphed, and I never rose from its ranks.

One year I was abroad in the fall, and during my
absence the gardener nailed a board over Tom's garage entrance. It was the end of October when I returned, and in the excitement of homecoming, and
the hurry of planting long overdue bulbs before the

snow came, Tom completely slipped my mind and I did not check to see that everything was in readiness for his coming. It was dusk when I came to the last six bulbs. I moved over to the hedge, and kneeling there with trowel poised, I became uneasily aware of some nearby presence — not ten feet away, his nondescript striped coat merging into the bare carrigana branches, was the malevolent battered face of Tom. But I recognized him only by the familiar cauliflower ears and lopsided snarl: there was a film over the usual malignancy in his yellow eyes, he was thin to the point of emaciation, and his swagger as he moved angrily away was a pitiful parody, for his hindquarters were dragging. I put out my hand and called to him, uselessly; he spat at me and crawled up the shelter of the hedge towards the garage. It was then that I discovered the gardener's inhospitable handiwork. I pried off the board and hurried away for food, upset beyond measure.

I made no attempt, then or later, to find out what had brought him to this desperate crawling state, or what the outcome would be, as I would have done with almost any other animal (and this respectful reticence was the only insensitivity of which I was not guilty in my relations with Tom). Then one morning there he was again, square and solid and sinister as ever, on his fence post. "Tom!" I cried winningly, rushing out with breakfast bacon in my hand, certain of my recognition at last, but the tattered ears flattened warningly, one long yellow fang appeared, and the contemptuous eyes dismissed me with a baleful blink. Humbled to my proper place again, I left my offerings in the garage.

He acknowledged me only once without a snarl. It was a night in late April, and the snow still lay in great drifts from a storm two days before. I woke in the darkness with the queer expectant urgency of being that has filled me ever since I can remember when I hear the first wild geese of spring or fall passing overhead. I thought I must have been dreaming, for it was too early for their return, and I had seldom heard them passing in the dark hours, but the familiar wild exhilaration was too strong to disregard. I opened the storm window as far as it would go and leaned out on the ledge; wisps of clouds were scudding across the moon, and the stars low on the horizon were enormous and bright in the predawn darkness. And then I heard that high, indescribable baying and yelping filling the skies, coming nearer and nearer. I ran downstairs and stood outside on the porch steps as they came, wild and exultant in the dark skies, and at that moment the moon broke through the clouds and I saw then that I was not alone to greet the hounds of spring: a few yards away on a stone pedestal flowerpot that rose clear of the snow, and that some passing hand had swept of its customary white mound, was a familiar hunched and solid silhouette, head upturned and eyes reflecting the moon's cold light. Together we listened and looked until the garden was empty and still again. I called to Tom then, and he turned his head and looked directly at me, and for once his ears did not flatten, and his eyes were without malice. He opened and shut his mouth several times, soundlessly, and I was close enough to see that he had very few teeth left. Then, as though aware of my sudden pity, he turned his back, jumped down onto the snow-swept path, and padded heavily off to the garage.

I never saw him again. His spring departure must have taken place that same morning, sudden and early as the geese. We sold the house shortly afterwards, moving only a few blocks away, and the end of that summer saw the dinghy upturned on its trestles once more in a new garage; but we were so close, the garage so like the other and at an approximating distance from the house, that I felt sure Tom would return to his stronghold, that he would seek it out because of the sustenance that went with it, and, even though indirectly, because of the humans who provided the sustenance. Hopefully I stowed an old kapok boat cushion under the upturned bows in October, pried two boards apart at the rear of the garage for easy access, and bought some cans of cat food.

But no villainous herald appeared before the first snowflakes; and the drifts around the garage lay unpatterned by paws throughout the winter; yet even as they sank before the April winds my foolish heart still leaped hopefully to every stripey prowler for miles around, and no heavy low-slung shadow ever padded down the lane that I did not think was Tom returned at last. But he never returned, nor was he ever seen at the old house.

I should have learned my lesson and known better than to hope for the return of something of which I had never owned a part. After four years' tuition I should have learned to recognize the unyielding snarl on the face of my tenant as being that of an honest cat; and the hospitable smile on mine as none other than that of the eternally hungry human tiger, insatiate for subjection, ravenous for tributary tidbits. Terrible Tom, that honest cat, must have seen the lurking tiger within as clearly as he recognized the kapok cushion, the cans of cat food, and the pried-open boards for the traps they were. The year would come when he no longer had the strength to spring them: rather than risk the ultimate humiliation, he avoided them for all time. And I, poor greedy tiger, blind to my own subservience, hunger by them still.

With Claud Beneath the Bough . . .

CLAUD is not even my canary: he belongs to my youngest daughter, and for nine and a half months of the year he is nothing more to me than a Noise, an automatic kitchen accompaniment to any running tap, whirring gadget, or boiling kettle. It is therefore quite possible to be entirely objective about this bird and admit that he has no more personality than any other canary: perhaps even less, for possibly there are tame, friendly, or even intelligent canaries: Claud is none of these. He has a pleasant enough voice, a little shrill perhaps early in the morning, but not in any way distinguished from a thousand others of his Harz Mountain relatives; nor is he in any way distinguished in his appearance, and I would not be able to pick him out in even a small canary identification parade: he is of standard banana color with a pointed beak, thin legs, and beady eyes like the ends of two black corsage pins — and as charged with expression. Towards the end of the school year the Noise gradually resolves into this visible form, appearing into view over my personal horizon like the ordained procession of a summer constellation, rising inexorably into a position of full feathered vocal magnitude, until, by the time the last examination is written, we are in conjunction. The force behind this is my daughter, who now wanes over the far horizon, her life too full and far-flung for Claud-inclusion; for better or worse, in moult or in plumage, until the end of summer do us part, I am stuck with Claud.

This has been my lot for three years now, so I look upon myself as almost a professional canary custodian, and as such feel qualified to warn any other innocent and conscientious parent who might accept a similar responsibility and embark on the job, as I once did, with the carefree idea that it is a daily task of a few minutes only: far from it — *the summertime care of a canary is a full-time occupation*, and is not to be entered upon lightly. There should be no delusions, for example, that feeding the thing is just a question of tipping some more seed into a semicircular plastic cup that hooks on to the bars. The well-equipped canary today — I am not, of course, discussing here underprivileged birds who tough it out with one packet of seed, newspaper on the floor and a saucer for a bird bath — comes with an extensive range of foods for it's extensive range of requirements: color, condition, song and egg output, moult, moodiness and general *joie de vivre* being among a few of these. There are Tuesday and Thursday extras, Monday,

Wednesday and Friday treats and tonics, vitamins to be squeezed in somewhere, and some may be given together and some may not. Much mental agony can be avoided by the novice parent by spending an hour or two at the beginning in making adequate charts on which items may be ticked off daily, and remembering that Saturdays and Sundays appear to be days of free enterprise so that anything really outstanding can be crammed in then. Cleaning the cage will be quite a shock at first to the uninitiated, too, for the canary is an almost pathologically untidy bird, with an insanely unbalanced ratio of mess to size, and capable of scattering seed to a distance forty times the length of its body. Anyone misguided enough at this point to imagine that these two basic tasks, feeding and cleaning, will make up the sum total of their daily activities is again in for a nasty shock: the rest of their day will be taken up with securing and rigging yet another hook to another tree or wall from which to suspend the cage; following the sun around to change its location; rushing home to take it in in case of rain; listening to it, sitting under a tree with it; encouraging, observing, and even on occasions walking around with it. However, this hectic life has many compensations to offer a dedicated canary custodian once the full magnitude of responsibility has been realized: it can be the most richly rewarding experience, and can open up hitherto undreamed of dimensions of living. . . .

Claud travels down from town for his summer holiday at a lakeside cottage in the back of the station wagon along with the dog, cat, hamster or any other current small animal or reptile. Over his cage (a splendid wicker pagoda-like affair) goes a custom-tailored turquoise plastic cape over which riot small purple parakeets and large pink tropical fish. This cape is essential on the journey so that he will not reel from his perch with vertigo occasioned by the continuous and rapid change of scenery, nor with hysteria at the message conveyed at six-inch range from the brilliant twin battery of sapphire Siamese eyes. His considerable luggage is in a canvas bag: boxes of seed, packets of fitted emeried paper to carpet his floor, at least six jars of variegated appetizers and tonics, his bath and personal shampoo, strings of millet, two cuttlefish and a Surprise Canary Joy Bell. Claud lacks for nothing. He is unveiled within the cottage, outwardly unchanged by his experience, debonair, unruffled, although it is significant that he does not say "Cheep." This could be stoicism or sulkiness; it could also be shock, so I take no chances, and he rests that first afternoon in the tranquillity of the cottage. If his nerves need any readjustment, now is the time for them to get on with it, for tomorrow they may be called upon to deal with mild agoraphobia when he becomes an Outdoor Bird once more after months of kitchen domesticity. He swings on his little trapeze with fathomless nonchalance.

His cage now is suspended from my No. 1 hook (brass curtain rail type) on a beam which runs across the living room ceiling, carefully chosen so that he enjoys an uninterrupted view of the lake on two sides, and at a height which enables him to see into the kitchen beyond the hatch, yet removes him sufficiently far from any table or piece of furniture whose proximity might put ideas into the head of an athletic cat; and, as there must also be some strategically placed obstacle to deter absentminded people from striking the cage with their heads and alarming Claud unduly, I have bolted a small footstool to the floor immediately below. This stool also makes a steady platform on which to stand when unhooking the cage, and may still be used for its original purpose if chairs are drawn up to it. Many hours of thought, observation and measurement went into the placing of that hook, and I mention it in detail, for there are seven other equally strategically planned hooks, wires or pulleys outside the cottage, and this may partially help to explain why the care of Claud in summer is such an all-consuming occupation. One is constantly adding to or improving upon them. For example, I sometimes wake up to find the lake a calm blue mirror, and feel that he would enjoy a morning suspended over its depths: this involves hitching the cage onto a clip hook (outboard motor safety chain type) spliced on to a line (see "Knots, Splices, and Fancy Work" for explicit instructions) that runs through a pulley wheel (from

redundant washing line) screwed on to a birch branch
(a perilous job) which extends over the water. The
tin tray on the floor of the cage is removed for this
operation so that Claud may look down through the
wicker slats and enjoy the reflection of himself if he
feels like it. I shall never know if he has felt like it.
Other hook sites are dotted around the property and
are used according to the prevailing wind that day,
or the weather forecast. Thus, if I have to leave him
for a while and the sky appears somewhat overcast
yet the day is still fine, he is suspended from No. 4
hook, a swivel one on a wire beneath the densely en-
twined branches of a spruce and birch that grow together. I estimate that only a very heavy continuous
rainfall of the thunderstorm type could penetrate this
cover, and naturally I would have battled back in my
sou'wester to rescue him long before such an eventu-
ality. This swivel hook (which I nearly forgot to say
came off a Brownie belt) has other advantages: the
cage twirls and swings from it in light winds, and
Claud therefore must take constant counter action if
he is not to perch in stationary nausea while in a
state of being twirled. He appears to enjoy this exercise (if one can estimate his pleasure by the fact that
he frequently jumps on his trapeze and swings from
it at the same time, apparently seeking added sensa-
tion), and I feel that its gentle insistency must be
excellent for semisedentary birds. But one must use
discretion and not overdo it: a canary with muscular,

overdeveloped legs would look ridiculous. In moderate winds I set the clockwork timer on the stove to Hard Boiled Eggs to remind me when to transfer him to Station 6, a stationary meathook on a sheltered ell of the cottage. This station is visible from the kitchen window, and is also the one at which he bathes every morning.

His bath is a kind of plastic annex that attaches to the door, like an observation dome, only sideways, and has two nonskid steps down into the water. But Claud is a prudish, modest bird, and will not enter his bath if he thinks he is being watched. Usually it is only possible to tell that bathing has actually taken place by the splash marks on the transparent plastic walls, and the evidence of fluff and seed floating on the surface of the water. I do not know why he should apparently eat in his bath, and thought it a rather disgusting habit at first, but have now decided that there is a lot to be said for this practice and have taken to eating overripe plums and watermelon in my own.

Claud's vacation day begins with mine, when I uncover him on rising. It is impossible to overlook uncovering him, for my bedroom is off the living room, and his cage hangs on my direct route through to the kitchen. It is therefore a foregone conclusion that two seconds after emerging through my door I will stub my toe on the bolted-down footstool, and will be reminded of Claud. After I have removed the cover I stare at him for a long time. I do not know why. Perhaps I am looking for signs of moult or hoping for an egg, perhaps I am searching his beak for some subtle change of expression, perhaps because I am just naturally a vacant, staring, vegetable thing first thing in the morning. I probably do not even see him, except that I have, somehow, a hazy idea that he looks a little frowsty first thing in the morning: untidy cage with seed thrown about all over the place, fluff in the corners and yesterday's apple slice brown, or lettuce limp and squalid. All I know is that I stare and stare with a glazed fixation, and suddenly he says "Cheep," but whether in fright, affection, loathing or hunger I do not know, and it is too early to care.

When I have rallied a little, after breakfast, I unhook the cage and carry it into the kitchen by the sink for replenishment and housecleaning. This event is always attended by the cat, and follows a set procedure: while I am washing the bath and various containers, his thin, clever, monkey-like paw is working away like a furry jimmy at the bamboo door which slides upwards in hatch fashion. Once he has his claws hooked under he manages to slide it up quite easily, but he has not yet been able to solve the problem that follows: one paw must always hold the door up, therefore to get the other into action for a Claud-clutching swipe through the aperture he must balance on his haunches like a squirrel, and this is out of the question, for I have not left him enough room on the counter. Next he tries holding the door up while inserting his head, but this is apparently anatomically impossible for a cat, and often leads to the door slamming down on his whiskers, which I enjoy very much, but which makes him more cross-eyed than ever with frustration. He slides the door up again and it is almost possible to see a balloon with "Thinks . . ." floating over his head. Claud watches enigmatically: he stretches a wing, looks under the tip as though checking on the time, then preens it, unconcerned. I pour myself another cup of coffee. Now the cat tries sliding his paw further into the cage so that the hatch door is supported on his elbow; he bends his head and sights along this paw as though it were a gun, and as he curls and uncurls the pads at the end the claws shoot in and out like flick knives. "Cheep," says Claud expressionlessly, turns his back and dips his beak into the Bis-kit in his Treet Kup. I bend down and sight along the cat's paw too: all I can see beyond the claws is an expanse of feathered yellow bottom curtsying up and down as its owner dips. Very tantalizing. I sympathize with the cat. Now the paw is retracted to position one, one negligent claw supporting the door; the cat crosses his eyes until they merge to an almost Cyclopean point and stares through the open door, presumably hoping to draw Claud like a magnet through it and into his unsmiling jaws. Dip, dip, goes Claud, insensitive as an oil derrick. I bend down again and sight along the opposite way this time, over the dipping yellow derrick and into the Eye beyond: what I see in its depths appalls me, no wonder Claud has turned his back upon it — naked, unashamed desire. This must be censored, so I turn the cold water tap on full blast: Claud springs automatically to the alert, whets his beak briskly against the bars, clears his throat in a preliminary trill or two, then drops into his customary elongated banana-like stance for vocal action: he sings at the top of his voice, with all rolling stops out. The cat reacts to this like a tiger confronted with a sheet of flames, or Sir Jasper foiled again in the melodrama: he winces and retreats, his offended ears flattened tightly to his head, the door hatch crashes down as he jumps off the counter and slinks away. Claud hurls trill upon blithe trill after, until at last I turn him off along with the tap: so much piercing cheer, so early in the day, is almost too much for me as well.

His seed cups are refilled now, a fresh carpet laid, his water replenished and his bath attached; six drops of some bottled elixir go into his drinking water, six hygienic drops from another bottle go into his bath water (and I think it might be reassuring to other canary sitters to know that I have — unintentionally — proved that a confusion in drops is harmless, which is reasonable when one thinks about it, for who is to stop a canary drinking its bath water or bathing in its drinking water?); and this is also a time to take the pliers to tighten the metal grips on cuttlefish, adjust perches, or surprise a canary by hanging its Surprise Joy Bell. (Claud reacted to his as though he had sent to know for whom it tolled, and fluttered around in his gravel with such obvious apprehension that I removed it.) This is also the time to make friendly overtures. . . .

It is a strange and mortifying fact that all the time that the cat's head is framed in Claud's doorway or that fearsome pronged paw is extended within his cage with obviously sinister intent, no trace of untoward emotion can be observed in Claud's behavior; but let my bountiful, philanthropic hand enter his cage, and he flaps around like some swooning Victorian heroine accosted in the conservatory, his feathered skirts huddled protectively about him, cheeping faintly — yet no hand has ever come near him save on benevolent purpose. My feelings are naturally hurt by this totally unwarranted response, so I devote some time to my overtures, with my hand inside the cage, the forefinger stretched out like a perch, hoping that he may in time calm down and alight upon it. I retain this position until my finger quivers like a compass needle; sometimes I tuck a piece of succulent lettuce between two fingers and say "Cheep, cheep," encouragingly; but he is never encouraged and is obviously going to have mild hysterics if I continue. It is at this point of our day together, the only point, that I feel a definite empathetic block in my relationship with this bird. "Cheep," he says with monotonous peeping plaint, pressed against his cuttlefish, "cheep . . ."

Weather permitting, while I am doing the dishes Claud's cage is hung at Station 6, the protected one, so that he will not be in a draught when he emerges from his bath, and so that I can lean over the sink and crane my neck sideways through the window and hope to catch him in the act. All that happens is that he cranes his neck sideways through the bars and watches me do the dishes. Yet the moment I leave the kitchen he apparently pops into his bath, and the only way I can trick him is by leaving the cottage by another door, creeping up quietly around the ell, then flattening myself against the wall to peep around; which is unsatisfactory, unsporting, and makes the milkman think me mad when rounding the corner himself.

By now it is mid-morning, and time for another cup of coffee, which I usually take to a rather boggy place at the end of our property where a large toad has lived for several years. He is often to be found sitting on a flat mossy rock at this time of day, look- ing like a portly guru in a suspended state of Om or Zen or whatever it is, his beautiful eyes unwinking and fathomless, apparently contemplating, for lack of a navel, space. I find him very restful, and restoring to my ego: he likes to have what passes for his chin tickled by the finger which has been so recently re- jected. Depending on whether he has bathed or not,

Claud — with whom I have not yet quite made it up — may or may not accompany me on this visit. If he does, his cage rests on a flat rock beside me, for there is no hook at this station; and, anyway I feel that it must be refreshing for him to see the world at ground level for a change. I contemplate the toad and the toad contemplates space, and we are silent; Claud does not contemplate anything, but cracks seeds and fidgets around his cage like some irritating occupant of the seat behind in a concert. Once he sang, which astonished the toad very much and roused him prematurely from his reverie. The length of our stay here is governed by both the state of the soles of my canvas shoes and the duration of the guru's trance: if he remains, rapt and unseeing, I remain until the bog seeps through to my socks; if he emerges from Om and hops ponderously away, I leave while my feet are still dry. The fact that my feet assume some importance here is probably why I so often find Claud's looming largely into my contemplative mind: his toenails seem unnecessarily long, they almost meet around the perch, and I do not know whether I should find a thicker perch or ask someone to cut them, but who? And why does he not just bite them himself? What better equipment for this than a beak? He wears a little bracelet on his left ankle, and often fiddles with it, turning it this way and that with his beak. . . . I do not like his feet. Sometimes the cat, who is an expert contemplater, materializes out of the jungle underbrush nearby and joins us. He and the toad appear to be on the best of terms. The cat contemplates Claud. Claud stuffs himself with seed indifferently.

By now it is noon probably, and I am usually able to tell what the weather is going to be like, and make my decision accordingly as to which hook it shall be for the long-time stay of the day. This summer has been a remarkably fine one, rather too hot for anything other than sunlight deflected through leaves, so Claud has spent most of his vacation among the lower branches of a giant birch between the lake and the cottage, at No. 3 hook, the clip off a spinnaker boom, which is attached to a wire between two branches. Below I have a full-length reclining chair and low table, and the nozzle of the hose is conveniently to hand should I feel like watering a far flower bed, driving off something, or stimulating Claud. The table is round and solid, and just the right size to hold a pair of binoculars, a field guide to birds, a wineglass, and a thermos jug, which I like to fill with a light, dry Niersteiner in my long-haired moments, tomato juice in my earthier. Here we have spent most of our days, and we have never lacked for company, whether it is his cage or his voice that attracts the audience. He responds to it like the professional he is and sings almost nonstop throughout the afternoons. Below, I am in a birdwatcher's paradise.

Even during intermissions it is a very sociable tree,

with room for all. Only a few feet above the cage is a robin's nest which has been occupied by two broods of gawping youngsters this summer, the last incubated, hatched and raised to the strains of canary music drifting up from below (this nest is an untidy, amateurish piece of housebuilding and appears to have been constructed from the contents of a wastepaper basket, as large pieces of Kleenex and scraps of wool have been rammed in here and there, and a piece of string hangs down like a bell pull — this causes Claud some inconvenience, as loose fragments frequently rain down on his cage). The robins are a pleasant friendly pair; I have a charming tape recording of him joining with Claud in a duet; while she is a talented ventriloquist — capable of issuing commands and warnings to her brood through a beak which remains snapped down firmly over three inches of despondent, looping worm. Various warblers flit about in the outer branches, which interrelate with other trees, and one of them, a myrtle, has provided us with some enthralling soap opera installments, being currently saddled with an oafish, spoiled, almost full-grown cowbird, whom she is apparently supporting on a widow's mite — for there is no sign of a mate. Every now and then her small harassed figure flits across the stage, the Widow Warbler, working her maudlin beak to the bone for her wastrel, outsize foster son, who lumbers after her from branch to branch, looming over her with hoarsely gaping insatiable beak. I am tempted to direct the hose into it. I have tried to help out by scattering some of Claud's seed around, but the Widow will have none of my charity.

Vireos make brief visits to our tree; various sparrow parents bring the youngsters along to practice take-offs and landings on the lower branches; nuthatch acrobats walk nonchalantly head foremost down the trunk; and two or three times a day a downy wood-pecker calls and taps his way up a branch with the preoccupied air of a housing inspector looking for signs of dry rot. There is never a dull or lonely moment.

I recline and sip the golden afternoons away. Some-times I rouse myself to record Claud's voice for pos-terity and hook the microphone of a tape recorder on to the bars of his cage. I resume reclining, my fin-gers on the knob at the ready. Up above Claud reacts in his usual suspicious temperamental way to any in-trusion of his cage, fluttering in protest, cheeping idiotically at the microphone as though it were going to attack him. I wait below, impassive and timeless as the toad, for some steady continuity of noise that will trigger his Pavlovian response. And if motorboats, power saws or passing helicopters fail to put in an appearance within a reasonable time I have another card up my sleeve: the sound of drumming water from the garden hose directed to an old pie plate nailed to the trunk of the tree is irresistible — Claud's professional reaction triumphs over his temperament and he performs. When I play his song back his reception is almost rudely indifferent: "Cheep," he comments stodgily, if he does not interrupt and sing the whole thing all over again in strident opposition.

Sometimes I feel that I have reclined and sipped so long that I have entered another dimension and have almost become part of the background. Twice now hummingbirds have investigated the red straw tassel on the top of my hat for nectar, and Mrs. Robin, her beak crammed revoltingly, sometimes takes a breather on my table before continuing upstairs to the nursery: the feathered world is moving in on me. Sometimes I sweep the binoculars around for glimpses into other domestic dramas being played out in nearby trees, or for individual identification of yet another member of the enormous warbler or sparrow family. And I think of how much I owe to Claud above for this increasing intimacy in feathered circles. Thanks to hours of summer togetherness and being watched at such close range by his many visitors, I no longer refer distantly to "that warbler" (or vireo or vulture), with the same social lack as one might say "that blonde" (or child or creep); but, with a modest offhandedness, I claim them now by such familiar terms as yellow-bellied, red-eyed, hairy, downy, or even three-toed. This could really make a party swing. And, thanks to Claud again, all this colorful name-dropping has been effortlessly achieved in the recumbent position. No perspiring pursuit down mosquito-ridden Nature Trails; no endless crouches or abortive stalks; no melting chocolate bar, or slaking of the thirst with tepid tea or muddy water; but a flask of wine, a loaf of bread (cut into the convenience of sandwiches), and Claud, beneath the bough, singing in the wilderness of unmown grass, weed-choked rock garden and shaggy hedge. All this conservation of energy that might have been expended, this sublime birdwatched inactivity, matches any Paradise I have read about, and has the added advantage of being obtainable without the usual preliminary qualifications of disembodiment. All this I owe to Claud too. Almost the only thing I do not owe him for is the Niersteiner.

There comes a time in late August when the slip-shod nest has long since been flown, and the yellowed leaves are already drifting down, when I gradually realize that Claud's vocal output is tailing off, and that there is a notable lack of confidence in the few selections now rendered. Then one day a yellow feather floats by with the down-drifting leaves; thicker and faster they fly with the days, these last feathers of summer, fewer and thinner the notes; until one day all is silence in the wicker pagoda and its occupant looks like a bird that never wert — Claud is down to one loose, dejected tail feather and the moths could have been at the rest of him. The summer is nearly over. Migrating birds are getting ready for the flight home to winter quarters; and so, somewhere, I hope, is my daughter. It is a good thing that Claud does not have to migrate, as he would not get very far in his present un-airworthy condition. Moulting at this time of year, it occurs to me, is a direct contravention of natural laws: Claud is either decadent or a rugged individualist. I suspect the latter.

There dawns the inevitable day. "Cheep," I say to him our last morning together, shocked into speech by a more than usually painful stubbing of my toe on the footstool, trying to cheer him up. "Cheep," I repeat, thinking that he looks as though I had played badminton with him all summer instead of lavishing care and atttention. "Cheep . . . ?" I am almost inhumanly jolly. Claud shrugs with languid indifference. He swivels his head backwards under a ravaged wing and examines the remnants of his tail structure with an inscrutable beak. He shrugs again, and the last presentable feather spirals gently down into his drinking water. I will add it to his other bookmarkers in my *Field Guide to Birds*.

Pas Devant le Chien

I BOUGHT a little electric heater for my workroom: pale turquoise with a slatted metal grille; and it very cleverly came on when the room grew cold, then switched off at the desired dialed warmth. The first afternoon I plugged it in it was resting quietly when Jonny wandered in, looking for someone to distract after a boring homework session with the nervous system of a frog. She lolled over my desk for some minutes, snapping the jaws of a stapler round the blotting paper, then: "What are you doing?" she asked. It was perfectly obvious what I was doing: sitting at a desk, writing a letter with a leaking ball-point pen. I have been campaigning against this barren, bootless type of question for years in the family, mainly with success, but with Jonny it seems to have deteriorated into a kind of verbal Snakes and Ladders, the rules undefined, yet each of us knowing perfectly clearly who has scored. My move: "I am walking down an up escalator, playing the bagpipes," I said, and licked a stamp squashingly, quite a feat in itself. "As you will, Mother," said Jonny equably, "although most people would think you were sitting at a desk, writing a letter with a leaking ball-point pen." She was going to play it cool. She leaned over my shoulder to read the letter — another habit I detest. "Dear Hermione," she started, and at that fatal moment the heater's fan purred into life.

"What's that?" she asked. Fair enough, it *could* be mistaken for a loudspeaker. "A heater," I said, and added, generously, "it heats the room." "Big news," said Jonny, "but how does it turn itself on like that?" She is seventeen, lives in a land of thermostats and passed physics last year. "There's a little man inside," I explained; "he lies on a tiny chaise longue, lightly dressed; and when he feels chilly he turns up the heat; and when he is all nice and warm again he turns it off. He is very sensitive."

"Oh, really?" said Jonny coldly.

If only she had retired now, chastened, to her frog; if only I hadn't — but I did: I leaned over and looked down into the grille with a fond smile, and I waved a tiny, intimate wave. And then heaven help me, I opened the door to the dial at the back, and lifted my tenant out. "Isn't he adorable?" I said, and smoothed back his hair as he sat on the palm of my hand.

"Ugh," said Jonny, then suddenly lunged and snatched him from me. She suspended him distastefully — by his arms, I suppose — between forefingers and thumbs, then twirled him rapidly round and round in the manner that expert grocers use to close paper bags. "How do you like *that*, you sensitive little man?" she asked, then threw him up to the ceiling and watched him fall, unmoved. I grabbed, but she pinned him down with a foot, then ground him very thoroughly into the carpet. "We don't want him to multiply, do we?" she said with a smugness that spurred me on down the fatal path. I gathered up the tiny remains, rearranged them, then restored him with a finger dipped in a cup of cold tea, ignoring Jonny's ostentatious wiping of the carpet. "Here's a leg," she said, smiling evilly as she handed it over — "and it's not his wooden one either," she added quickly, forestalling me. I screwed the leg back on with a hairpin, outwardly nonchalant. "You see," I said triumphantly, "he's as good as new again — "

"I'd like to shake his little hand — " said Jonny; but she moved towards me with such a predatory look that I swiftly popped him back into the Tom Tiddler's ground of the heater. She kneeled beside me and peered into the grille. "He looks shocked," she said accusingly, "you put that leg on backwards — "

I was just about to make a tacit admission of defeat by saying that I had no further use for him anyway, and then returning to my letter, when a third head thrust its way in between us, and a third pair of eyes stared intently down the grille. We had forgotten all about him: he had followed Jonny in, and must have witnessed the whole terrible scene from his lair under the table — stout, immensely respectable and elderly, a most dogged dog, he had taken everything to his zealous heart. He has a loosely fitting coat with a lot of surplus material, several folds of which were now puckered into deep thoughtful furrows all over his face. His honest eyes shone with the sincerity of his belief, his ears fairly quivered with anticipation: something lived in that new cage — it had been taken out, made much of, massacred, restored — *and put back in again*. He could not yet see it, but with application, resolution and vigilance he would: today, tomorrow, it mattered not. He would wait. He had plenty of time.

Our hearts sank under his solid weight of purpose. We knew it too well. A small example: throughout the day he sleeps at the top of the stairs; they are narrow, he is not; for nine years he has been trodden on, tripped over, cursed, threatened, dragged away, prodded, Hoovered; he has many breakfasts and countless cups of coffee spilt over him on Sundays. He is there at this very moment. "I must return to my frog," said Jonny uneasily; and left me, well and truly hoist.

An hour later he was still staring in, his absorption fanned into white-hot intensity at excitingly irregular intervals. I turned the switch off, but silence was apparently even more suspenseful. I unplugged it and shoved it under a loveseat; as much of him as could immediately manage disappeared after, his voluminous white knickerbockers heaved, the seat teetered drunkenly for a minute, then settled down, panting

audibly and wagging a long feathered tail. Even Jonny
was appalled when she saw what we had done: it was
as bad as some well-meaning but confused adult
searching the night skies with field glasses for airborne reindeer on Christmas Eve, she said pointedly.
I thought that probably the parent had been driven
into understandable confusion by the constant asking
of idiotic questions by its children. Score equal.

We locked the heater into a cupboard: he lay like
a Landseer with his nose to the crack, whining. We
unscrewed the back and showed him the exposed
innards: he settled down to his vigil wearing the
heater on the front half of his head. We lured him
down to his dinner and tried smuggling it out in a
suitcase during his absence, but he tracked it out to
the garage, and flopped as possessively on the suitcase as though it had a recent headstone at one end.
We climbed a ladder and thrust it through the attic
trapdoor in the ceiling: he threw his head back and
howled below. We could not settle down to anything. At midnight we threw in the sponge, put the
heater in his basket and went to bed, leaving him
gazing rapturously into its depths.

His whiskers were wilted with sleeplessness next
morning, his eyes drooping halfway down his face —
but the same fanatic light still burned as bright as
ever in their depths. I was torn between compassion
and a strong desire to short-circuit the heater and
shock him back to his senses. But Jonny thought this

should only be done as a last resort. She suggested that as I had tenanted the little turquoise home in the first place I was technically the landlady: I should now use the same convincing powers to evict my tenant. So I plucked the poor little man out, not once but a dozen times, and we took turns in disposing of him under the watchful eyes of the dog: he was thrown out of the window, buried, drowned in breakfast cereal, flushed away, posted, and returned to the milkman in an empty bottle. Jonny finally made a sandwich out of him and took him to school for lunch. Each method was attended to its tragic end by the dog, who would then reel back to his post at the source.

I spent a profitless day with the sleep-starved victim of my pedantic folly. I borrowed a long-playing bear that tinkled Brahms' Lullaby when a knob in its stomach was pressed; I sat it on the heater, then drew the blinds and tiptoed into cover — hoping he might drop off so that I could snatch the heater, and he would wake up and think he had dreamed the whole thing. This made me think, when I woke myself up later, of a friend who is a retired psychiatrist and has a pack of decidedly neurotic poodles. I rang him up, long distance too, and explained our problem. *Very,* very interesting, he said, after a long expensive pause, it was a classic case of Canine Fixation. The patient's suspense must be relieved: attempting to relieve it by the negation of nonexistence was a negative approach:

positive substitution was indicated. In other words, he explained in bright kindly tones, murdering little male thermostats meant nothing to a dog, we must install instead a *real* little tenant in our heater. He said that he was sorry, sizewise, that he was not able to move in himself, it sounded cozy; but he thought that there must be plenty of tenant material at the Bottom of the Garden if we inquired around, or knocked on the doors of a few toadstools — with this present cold spell as an added inducement there must be many who would be only too delighted to move into a heated apartment. We might consider Lilliput too . . . ideal recruiting ground . . . probably direct jet service there nowadays . . . I promised to send him a postcard if there was, and hung up discouraged: if this was a *professional* reaction —

When Jonny returned late that afternoon Old Faithful had been without sleep for twenty-four hours — twenty-two more than his usual daily quota — and he looked it: disheveled, sagging, reeling in his tracks. So was I. I was ready to give my brand-new heater away — it was by now too battered to return — or hurl it into the lake, pound it to pieces with a sledge hammer — But Jonny, refreshed after an eight-hour absence, pointed out that the results of sudden heater-deprivation might be even more traumatic: he might spend the rest of his life keening round the house like some hairy banshee, looking for it. The Poodle Doctor's idea of a genuine occupant really added up —

"Then wing off to Never-Never Land with him and find one," I said querulously, "and before you go pour me a long, strong drink." "Do you mind if I take the car instead?" she said. "The nursery window's stuck."

She returned within an hour, modestly triumphant. "We'll leave Him in the car until H Hour," she said. H Hour was 6:30 — Old Faithful's dinnertime. At 6:29 he dragged himself away from the heater to fortify himself for the night watch. His bowl, well greased on the underside, awaited him on the skiddy kitchen tiles, its contents mixed into a glutinous delaying paste. Jonny tore out to the car and then upstairs. Ten minutes later he lurched through the doorway, heading blearily for the heater. I unscrewed the back, and he watched with polite interest. Then Jonny inserted her hand and slowly drew out a fat, placid hamster, clutching a peanut in its pink hand. It gazed benignly down on the astounded furrowed face below, and crammed the peanut into its bulging cheeks. The dog was enchanted; in a quivering ecstasy he watched Jonny open the door of a neat green cage with a kind of treadwheel inside. He rested his head on the table, his nose against the bars, his besotted eyes following the hamster as it waddled around, inspecting the larder, doing a few press-ups on the bars. He positively doted when it scratched its ear. It curled up in a corner in a snug ball, yawned hugely, and fell asleep. A minute later there was another cavern-

ous yawn, and the dog slowly folded into a vast in-
animate heap under the table.

It has been the most successful substitution. Godot,
the hamster, sleeps most of the day, leaving the dog
free to get his own head down at the top of the stairs,
or check the dustbins, etc. In the evening he delights
the dog with a performance of acrobatics. Last thing
at night he has a run round the workroom, and does
some intrepid mountaineering up the loose sliding ter-
rain of his infatuated owner. The heater heats, turning itself on and off, untenanted, ignored.

Yesterday Jonny came into the kitchen when I was
frying some bacon and eggs, the dog in hopeful at-
tendance. "What are you doing?" she asked. "I am
mixing some cement for. . . ." I started automatically,
then caught her eye: *"Pas devant le chien — "* she said
with a priggish wag of her finger. "I am frying two
eggs and four rashers of bacon in a frying pan," I said
humbly.

William

S INCE early morning, when he had awakened the household with his imperious whining, the dog whose name was William had been restless and had craved incessant attention with all the privilege of his fifteen years: he importuned first one with his insistent bullethead, and then another with a demanding paw; he whined to be let out, then almost at once demanded readmittance; and always there was a strange puzzled intentness of appeal in the questioning ears and in the depths of his small almond eyes.

The children of the family were very patient: they did not scold him when he lay down on the floor in the midst of their game of Racing Demon and his pleased tail scattered the piles of cards; when, slowly and stiffly, he rolled over onto his back in the preliminary to a game they had almost forgotten, they accepted the invitation — they bent over him in turn, daring him, then shrieked triumphantly "Missed again!" as he snapped with finely calculated error at their noses. Later, when the rain stopped at last, they set off on their bicycles, their young retriever run-

ning behind; but halfway up the winding drive one
of them had looked back and seen a white figure
plodding determinedly after. They waited for him
then, and walked very slowly, pushing their bicycles
to his pace. Very soon, however, he had tired and sat
down, mulish ears laid back, eyes slitted protestingly.
They had come only a short distance from the cottage, so the children pointed back and told him firmly
to go home; he drooped his head and allowed one
leg to shiver pathetically so that their hearts were
touched; they left their bicycles at the side of the
road and walked back with him. Usually when he
had scored some point like this he was immediately
transformed with gaiety, but today he did little more
than stir his tail apathetically. When he sat down
again, halfway home, the eldest picked him up without comment and carried him into the cottage.

The wide windows of the living room looked out
over the lake, the low white ceiling was bright with
the rippling reflections of sunlit waves, and the thin
curtains billowed gently before a fresh light breeze
that brought a heady, rain-washed potpourri of clover
and thyme, mint and wild roses into the room. The
terrier sniffed appreciatively, then climbed into his
basket, which the children had moved into a warm
patch of sun. One of them picked a sweet pea from
the bowl on the table and dropped it in beside his
nose for his additional pleasure. They filled his water
dish, patted him affectionately, and left.

He fell asleep at once, the waves slap-slapping a cheerful accompaniment to his gentle snoring. But all too soon he woke, whining softly, to resume his restless wanderings. At last he pushed open the screen door and ambled down to the shore, where he lay in the shallow water and lapped in a desultory way at the little waves breaking against his nose. Presently he left the water, barked from long custom at the insolent sea gulls on the raft, then settled down by a favorite young apple tree to wait for the children's return. They rode quickly when they came, for one of them carried an already melting ice cream cone. She kneeled on the grass beside him, turning the cone as he licked his painstaking way around, but halfway down he turned his head away, and the cone was tossed to the waiting retriever. They teased him afterward with long grass stalks, tickling his sensitive ears and dropping clover on the long down-arched nose, for they loved to watch him clasp his paws tightly around in protection, his cunning dark eyes peeping out between, bright with humor. The young retriever watched hopefully from a few feet away, but when he was about to move over to participate in the fun he was warned off with a despotic, pettish growl and stopped in his tracks.

It seemed this day that some newly developed need turned the terrier to the children, although for many years now they had outgrown the almost proprietary

interest he had shown in each of them since birth. He
had continued to be possessive and jealous if they
displayed too much affection for the newcomer within
the house, although he seemed to recognize their need
for a younger, more active companion outside; he
was like an elderly nanny who sees that her brood
has grown beyond nursery care, yet still exerts her
discipline. And they, who had pulled themselves up
in turn from the ground to their first steps by his
tender ears and patient tail, who had poked explora-
tory fingers into his loving eyes and turned back his
pink lips to examine his shining teeth, were now as
tolerant and patient as he had been with them.

In the early afternoon they left their own young
dog behind and took William with them in the sailing dinghy, unable to withstand his wistful expression
when he saw the picnic bag brought aboard. He was
no longer certain of his balance in a heeling boat, so
they wedged him securely between their knees. But
in a short time the boat was at the end of the dock
again; he was very unhappy, the children explained
— whining and looking back always to the shore.
They helped him out, and he stumbled up the dock
in anxious haste, and there at the end he came upon
a wooden garden chair, so low that his head was level
with the arm.

He laid his muzzle along the arm and stood there,
searching the face of the occupant. And she who had
lived a decade and a half of her life in his company,

looking back at him now, patting him in welcome, would not admit in her heart that this was an old dying dog but sought only to justify his desperate weariness by saying that this sultry weather would make anyone tired. And when the eldest child said, almost pityingly, "Mother, there is something wrong when William is not hungry —" she would not even then come halfway toward the admittance of truth but remarked only on the healthy coldness of his nose. And when the youngest, blunt with impersonal honesty, said, "Of course, he is really *ancient*, isn't he?" her mind sidetracked this issue too, and she reminded them only of great Argos and of Wassie, their grandfather's dog, who had lived for seventeen rat-catching years.

She looked down fondly as she spoke, seeing only the familiar recognition in his eyes, shutting her mind to their bluing blindness. But the children saw a thin-necked, frail dog with stiff, sinking hindquarters and trembling legs. They called their young retriever, and he leaped into the dinghy with flailing exuberance. Once more they set off for their picnic, released from uneasy pity.

Their mother watched them go, the dog leaning against her knee, her hand absently turning one of his ears inside out and back again. Small cat's-paws of wind frisked over the water to tinkle the sheep-bells hanging from a nearby birch; an ax rang against wood from somewhere across the bay and was silent

again; the children's voices receded. Soon the red sails
were out of sight, and the lake was quiet and empty
once more. A fish rose with a small plop off the end
of the dock, and even before the circles had gone,
there was another and another. Presently a reel
whirred and a line snaked out over the water; five
minutes later the dog pinned a small, flapping perch
down with an experienced paw and held it there until
the hook was removed and the perch dispatched. He
picked it up by the tail, then followed with slow
importance up the steps and into the cottage, the fish
dangling from his mouth. The screen door banged to,
almost defiantly, behind them.

By evening the wind had risen until the lake was
wild and stormy again under scudding black clouds,
and the rain lashed at the windows; the gulls soared
screaming over the birch tops in the gusts of wind
that rattled the doors and spattered the rain down the
wide chimney to sizzle on the log fire. The lamps
were lit early, and when darkness closed out the wild
night the streaming windowpanes reflected only a
tranquil softly lit room, undulating gently in the rivulets. The children finished at last a seemingly endless,
involved game with counters and dice spread all over
the floor; then they made hot chocolate, and popcorn
on the fire. They offered some to the terrier, who normally relished a saucer of chocolate and as much popcorn as he could hypnotize out of anyone, but tonight
he could not be persuaded, although he accepted a

lump of sugar soaked in rum from the hand that had first given him this strange treat when he had been desperately ill as a puppy, and his nose and lips wrinkled with the same shocked delight at the strong rum fumes as they had many years ago.

This memory touched a responsive, reminiscent mood in the children, sprawled contentedly before the fire; as they occasionally appealed to their mother for verification, the familiar enchantment of "I remember when — " took hold of them.

The span of their conscious remembrance stretched back across the years and half a world away to a rambling old house in the south coast country of wartime England; stretched back to a time when they were so small that sometimes tonight they had a sudden catch of memory, involuntary as a catch of breath, but holding such intriguing promise that they felt if only they could grasp the fleeting second an instant longer they would remember the secret of something more important, of a time before life even. "I remember, I remember," they said, their brown faces flushed in the firelight and tense with concentration. "I remember, I remember, too," echoed their mother silently from the shadowed depths of a chair beyond the pool of light, and she marveled that their perspectives of memory could project such different images.

The voices rose and fell, and the terrier slept in the security of their midst, no longer restless and demanding attention, unaware that he was receiving now the fullest recognition of all in a world of retrospect, where his identity emerged as many-sided as the facets of memory reflecting it.

The childhood world was one of endless summer, it seemed: where you went to bed when the sun still shone and rose to find it still shining, and only the nightingale singing in the cherry tree wakened you to look out and see the miracle of a moon-drenched garden through eyes just clearing the level of the nursery windowsill; where your burdens were few and light — tapioca pudding and the skin on tepid cocoa being among the heaviest; and under the dining room table sat a discreetly invisible ally, loyally sharing them. . . . Upstairs in the nursery world the children slept at night, undisturbed and calm, but downstairs was the other world of a blacked-out house in a darkened country, strained and haunted by absence; the creeping oppression and utter silence of the endless evenings, shared only by the dog lying curled in the armchair opposite — a dog who must listen to the interminable Chronicles of Barsetshire (because the voice that reads must break the silence somehow or be stifled by its weight), whose tenor howl alone joins with the giggling soprano at the piano and sends the offended silence fairly scurrying into the night before the duet of "Afton Water," who is always willing to lead the way down to the abysmal dark of the coal cellar, who fears not bats or mice, and whose teeth gleam reassuringly until the footsteps are identified.

A childhood world of delightful absurdity where, tabletop small, you could yet look down into the strange anemone eyes of giant farm horses, because their great necks arched over into your garden at ground level while they stood on their field that dropped away below; a sunlit, fragrant world of blackberrying in the hedges of those vast fields that stretched forever from that garden — purple-stained faces and hands, sunbonnets and sandals, and a purple-mouthed dog who enjoyed blackberries too, whose tail thrashed the basket from your scratched hands, who was ever valiant with cows. . . . But in the other world those same vast fields were small, too small and vulnerable, that still summer evening when the first obscenely sputtering black birds of war wobbled low across them and sickened the mind of one who watched with the as yet unguessed purpose of their evil; but before it had time to grow, the loneliness of fear had been dispelled by the furious wild barking of the indignant custodian of those fields, who had erupted out of his house and given chase, racing through the hedge and across the churchyard, hurdling the gate into the fields beyond, barking defiance at the monstrous bird until it sputtered redly out of his range and the staccato barking of the batteries beyond took up his cause, whereupon he had turned his back upon it and with the most expressive dismissal at his command, lifted his leg against a fence post. . . .

One world of breathless excitement where a gigantic rabbit with ruby eyes called Nigel romped in acres of orchard with a marmalade cat as big as a tiger called Daniel and a huge, whirling dog called William, scattering a thousand enormous hens among windfalls never equaled since in juiciness; and you drew a terrible face on a brown paper bag stuffed with straw on the end of a stick and scared the greedy starlings off the ripening fruit; and for this you received a penny, and another for that same William who had assisted but had no pockets of his own. . . . And another world, where children's gas masks, dolefully camouflaged into a goitrous cross between Mickey Mouse and an anteater, hung by the cellar door; and an infant-sized dog obligingly deputized for the trial run of a "Helmet, anti-gas: Infants, for the use of," as supplied by a benevolent government, breathed the air pumped in by a hand bellows with such reassuring affability that he had looked, to the now suddenly hilarious audience that peered through the plastic window, exactly like the Duchess's Pig Baby. . . . The apples that year were small and sour, foxes made off with six of the twelve hens, and Nigel got into the vegetable garden.

"I remember, I remember," said the children of those distant years when horizons stretched no further than the blue blur of sea glimpsed from the breathtaking heights of the Downs, those hills across whose springing turf you raced at the heels of your dog after a long-tailed kite, the dragon soaring and curtsying before the cloud shadows, the meadowlarks filling the skies with delight. . . . "I remember, I remember, too," silently echoed their mother of a distant, never to be forgotten dawn on those same hills, when the horizon that stretched across that blur of sea was the waiting coast of France; and a young woman and her dog, with only the sleepy stirring sheep to share their vigil, had waited in the predawn darkness until they had heard at last, not meadowlarks, but the steady droning increase of a thousand engines; and they had seen, not dragon kites, but line upon endless line of mighty bombers towing behind them long tails of silent gliders, and with myriad proud lights in the paling skies a great airborne armada swept majestically over the last little hills of England and across the coast to France and the dawning of a new day. It had been too much for the infinitesimal being to witness alone; the indifferent sheep moved off, and the patient bullet-head of the dog soaked up the warm spontaneous tears of pride and hope and exultation, and the slow corroding ones of grief and pity were already welling up and would surely have fallen too had he not struggled free before them to celebrate the miraculous new day with more suitable emotion. He had raced in mad exhilaration around her, barking joyfully, until at last the infection of his mood brought her to her feet and she raced him down the hill, scattering the rabbits, stampeding the cold-eyed sheep, flying down the chalky tracks, and rolling down dew-wet slopes in a whirling world of sky and grass, shadows shortening in the rising sun. . . .

"Bedtime," she said at last, still breathless and laughing from the descent, and moved her numbed foot from under the same bullethead that had struggled free from the bitter salty threat of morbid emotion, years — or was it minutes? — ago. "Bedtime," she said, more firmly.

But the long day was not yet over; in the middle of the night she was startled out of sleep by the cold brilliancy of a lightning flash, followed almost immediately by a tumultuous clap of thunder overhead. Her eyes screwed up tightly, her heart pounding, she waited for the agitated scratch at the door that must surely follow, for she and the terrier shared a deep and shameful secret; they were cowed and abject to the very marrow of their bones before a thunderstorm. They had accepted with reasonable detachment in their time the earth-shaking crumps of mortal thunder and its accompanying murderous lightning and had never lost a night's sleep lying awake to worry about it, but one small distant rumble of celestial thunder in the night reduced both to craven curs, sharing a bed of misery, with blanket-muffled ears.

But no sound or movement in the cottage followed; with a sudden dread that overcame all other, she went

in search of her companion in fear. She saw him in
the next searing flash — huddled and still, on his side
under the table in the far corner of the room. She
slid him out along the floor, then carried him over to
the sagging old sofa by the fire, where she wrapped
him in a blanket. Working swiftly, not daring to think,
she lit a candle, found eggs, brandy, and sugar,
switched them together, and poured some down his
unresistant throat. His ears and muzzle were cold and
she rubbed the blanket to and fro across his body,
then kneeled and looked closely into his eyes for the
spark of recognition, of life; it was there — in the very
depths, but there — and she rubbed more vigorously.
Presently he grew warmer, the pink tinge returning
to his ears, nose, and eyes; in her relief she took his
head between her hands and laid her cheek to it.

She put another log on the fire and watched the
flames curl up the birch bark; in their comforting
light she returned to the sofa, slipping her bare feet
under the shared blanket against his returning warmth.
He lay there peacefully, his head on her lap, and his
eyes wide open, yet far away and dreaming. Beyond
the windows the storm was subsiding at last, and together, for the first time without fear, they listened
to the grumblings of a thunderstorm in retreat across
the lake. The moon sailed free from ragged clouds
and lit the dinghy dancing at its buoy. In the pale light
she leaned over the old dog: his eyes gleamed in sudden amusement; then a split second later came the

soft click of teeth a fraction off the end of her nose. "Missed!" she said exultantly, laughing down at him, and at the sound of her voice his tail moved briefly under the blanket. She lay back against the cushions, smiling. "*Good* dog," she said after a minute, and then, still smiling, fell asleep. He stirred a little, sighed deeply, and slipped as easily into sleep.